OFF THE ROAD

*20 Rides for Mountain Bikes
in Central Southern England*

PHIL BAKER

GW00507569

DOVECOTE PRESS

Phil Baker lives in Basingstoke and started cycling off-road in the spring of 1990 when, while walking the Dorset Coastal Path, he hired a mountain bike to cycle to Hardy's Monument. The absence of tried and tested routes in book form led him to begin developing routes around his native region along the South Coast. In 1992 he gave guided tours of these rides to small groups, which has culminated in *Off The Road*.

First published in 1993 by the Dovecote Press Ltd
Stanbridge, Wimborne, Dorset BH21 4JD

ISBN 1 874336 13 X

© Phil Baker 1993

Phototypeset in Bembo by The Typesetting Bureau
6 Church St, Wimborne, Dorset
Printed and bound by Biddles Ltd,
Guildford and King's Lynn

While every attempt has been made to choose routes along known public rights of way for bicycles, this cannot be guaranteed. Although suitable places for car parking have been indicated, no responsibility can be taken for any fines or damage to the vehicle caused by parking there.

CONTENTS

INTRODUCTION

Selecting the Routes

Choosing the right route can make all the difference between an enjoyable day out and a disastrous time; it is the difference between a long descent on a firm chalk track, and wading ankle deep through a muddy bog.

However, finding a route suitable for off-road cycling is not as straightforward as one might imagine. Just because a track or bridleway is marked on a map, that is no guarantee it is possible to cycle. It may be overgrown with brambles, causing punctures; or it may be too muddy or rutted to cycle, requiring you to get off and walk; or the surface may be of loose gravel, making it dangerous to brake. And often one way round a circular route is easier than the other, due to the gradients. It can be more than annoying to find that you have spent the entire ride cycling uphill. My first attempts at off-road cycling resulted in problems finding the route, impassable ways, and the inevitable punctures from cycling on inappropriate terrain. The rides in this book avoid these pitfalls, giving the reader a tried and tested route to follow.

In this book, I have compiled 20 circular rides across what I consider to be some of the best countryside in an area of Southern England from Chichester to Weymouth. These range between 12 and 38 miles in distance, and within each ride I have tried to list a choice of routes to satisfy all cycling abilities. My experiences have shown that 12 miles is a suitable distance for those starting out, while 16 to 18 miles provides a good day's exertion for the casual cyclist. The longest routes in excess of 30 miles are sufficient for even the fittest enthusiast.

The routes combine a mixture of off-road tracks and quiet country lanes that provide exciting, yet not too extreme, cycling.

Equipment: the bike and what to take

It is possible to cycle any of these routes on an "All-Terrain Bike" (ATB). You do not need to spend hundreds of pounds on specialist equipment; provided your bicycle is reasonably rugged, it will cope with the rides described here.

You will need a water bottle, even if it is not hot. It is surprising how thirsty you will become cycling uphill, and having a water bottle handy will avoid you suffering from dehydration. Punctures are the bane of cycling off-road and you should always carry a pump, a puncture repair kit and tyre levers, spanners and Allen Keys if your bike requires them. It is advisable to carry a spare inner tube, since it is much easier to replace an inner tube at the roadside than mend the puncture. I have found that the use of a tyre liner, such as "Mr Tuffy" which fits between the tyre and inner tube, drastically reduces the number of punctures caused by thorns.

In general it is best to load up the bike rather than yourself. There is a whole host of luggage equipment available, but you will find that you can squeeze most essentials into a simple "Shoulder Holder" that fits on the crossbar. A "Dirt Bag" which fits behind the saddle, in much the same way as the old-fashioned saddle bag, will provide useful carrying space for such items as maps, compass and cagoule. If you do not mind spoiling the lines of your bike, a rack that fits over the rear wheel is perhaps the most versatile luggage item. It also has the added advantage of acting as a rear mudguard.

There are two types of carrier for transporting your bike. One type carries bikes on the roof of the car, while the other hangs bikes over the rear bumper. The latter type of carrier is probably more convenient, and despite any initial reservations you may have about whether it will stay hooked to the car, you will find that once these carriers are firmly strapped down they are surprising rigid. Be sure that the loaded bikes do not obscure the view of your number plate, brake lights and indicators, since this is illegal as well as dangerous. If your bikes are transported on the roof of your car, be wary of car park entrances with height restrictions! With some cars (larger hatchbacks in particular), it is possible to put one or two bikes inside by removing the front wheel and turning the handlebars in line with the frame.

5

Equipment: what to wear

Deciding what to wear appropriate to the weather conditions on the day is always difficult. It is surprising how much heat you will generate when cycling up an incline, but how cold it can be on a descent over exposed downland. Standing in the car park at the start of the ride, you will probably over estimate the clothing needed to keep warm. However, if in doubt, wear extra clothing: You can always remove it.

When it is hot, a T-shirt and shorts may suffice. A wind-proof top is an invaluable item since it will keep you warm without being bulky, and if rain is possible take a lightweight waterproof cagoule. In cooler weather, wear shellsuit bottoms adding a sweatshirt if need be. For more extreme conditions there is specialist clothing available, though I have found a ski-jacket is an effective alternative since not only is it warm, windproof and showerproof, but it can be unzipped to prevent overheating.

Always choose light, flexible footwear with a rugged sole. Nylon hiking boots or Trainers are ideal. Gloves are a useful accessory, since exposed hands can become very cold. Shatterproof eye protection is advisable to guard from mud, stones and insects (good plastic sunglasses are suitable). The use of safety helmets is a more personal matter: A helmet certainly gives an added sense of security when going downhill, but can be cumbersome when cycling uphill.

Using this Book

There is a complete variety of rides in this book. The routes range from easy cycling along fairly flat well-defined tracks in North Hampshire, to steep uphills on rough grass at Cerne Abbas and the Purbeck Hills. There are rides in popular off-road cycling areas such as the South Downs and New Forest as well as others in lesser known areas of Dorset such as Ibberton Down and Pentridge Hill.

The description for each ride follows a set format in order that the reader is given consistent directions. Against the distance for each of the routes within a ride I have stated the approximate time I believe it will take to complete that route. This is the time needed to cycle it with only the minimum of rests, based on my own tour of that route. On the surface you may feel the time looks a little generous, but bear in mind that when cycling off-road you will only cover about 6 miles in an hour.

The route descriptions give an indication of what the ride entails and what is on the route. This will allow you to determine whether a particular ride is suitable for your trip. By concentrating the narrative here I have been able to give more concise directions, hopefully making them easier to follow when riding.

I have tried to ensure that there is suitable parking at the start point of each ride. Where possible I have used appointed car parks with enough room for unloading, to leave the car. Since it is important to get off to a good start, I have given instructions to reach the start venue from an easily identifiable point.

The rides follow a circular pattern and are presented in the form of two outward stages and a return stage. In order to make the return stage as interesting as the rest of the ride, I have not re-used the outward route. The route directions give the best way round to cycle to avoid uphill gradients, and where there are steep uphill sections these are notified. I have avoided cycling uphill to start with believing it is better to "warm up" before tackling these, though this sometimes leads to an uphill section at the end of the day. I have also drawn attention to muddy sections so that you can either avoid them or seek them out, depending on your preference!

Mountain biking is about cycling off-road. Of the four off-road rights of way, it is legal to cycle on all except footpaths. Therefore I have based my routes around Bridleways, Roads used as a public path (RUPP's) and Byways open to all traffic (BOAT's). However, it is generally necessary to take to the road in order to complete a circular route. For this I have avoided using main roads and roads where the traffic is busy, choosing quiet country lanes on which to cycle. I am sure that you will find these enjoyable to cycle in their own right.

Along with the route directions, I have mentioned possible stopping places, picnic places and pubs. The emphasis on pubs is that they are usually the most convenient places to rest in the countryside. I have given an indication of what type of food is available so that you can make provision for this. A word of warning regarding leaving your bike in pub car parks: don't! A muddy bike receives no respect from motorists. I always take my bike into the garden, and lock it to a bench if going inside.

I have attempted to give sufficient information in the sketch maps so that it is possible to follow the route by these, without necessarily buying Ordnance Survey maps to cover the area. These maps are not to exact scale, since they are designed to give enlarged detail around junctions for clarity. For those who may wish the additional detail provided by a map, I have given the appropriate OS Landranger series sheet number that covers the ride together with a grid reference for the start point.

The Mountain Biker's Code of Conduct

The Countryside Commission and the Sports Council have developed a code of conduct for cycling off-road, the details of which are reproduced below:

1 Fasten all gates.
2 Leave no litter.
3 Guard against all risk of fire.
4 Keep to public rights of way for bicycles (do not ride on footpaths).
5 Stay on the trail, especially across farmland.
6 Use gates and stiles to cross fences.
7 Make sure your bike is safe.
8 Always wear a helmet
9 Follow the Highway Code.
10 Give way to walkers and horse riders.
11 Moderate your speed.
12 Cycle in control. Do not skid
13 Warn others of your approach.
14 Make no unnecessary noise.
15 Know where you are going!

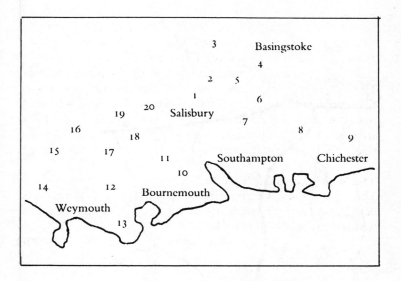

Summary of the Rides

Ride	Terrain	Distances	Town nr Start	Best Attributes
1	moderate	14, 19, 31	Winchester	all-round
2	easy	12, 31	Winchester	starters
3	easy	13, 17	Andover	starters
4	moderate	19	Basingstoke	off-road
5	easy	15, 19, 32	Basingstoke	countryside, villages
6	moderate	13, 20, 38	Winchester	Alresford, Itchen
7	moderate	13, 18	Winchester	all-round
8	difficult	16, 22	Chichester	off-road
9	moderate	12, 17	Chichester	off-road, woods
10	easy	15	Southampton	New Forest
11	easy	15	Southampton	New Forest
12	moderate	13, 17	Bournemouth	heath & woodland
13	difficult	14, 21	Bournemouth	sea views, beach
14	moderate	16, 23	Weymouth	countryside, Abbotsbury
15	difficult	18	Dorchester	off-road
16	moderate	16, 18	Blandford	all-round
17	easy	16, 22	Blandford	Badbury Rings
18	difficult	18, 22	Salisbury	off-road
19	moderate	18, 36	Salisbury	countryside, villages
20	moderate	12, 16, 21, 36	Salisbury	countryside, villages

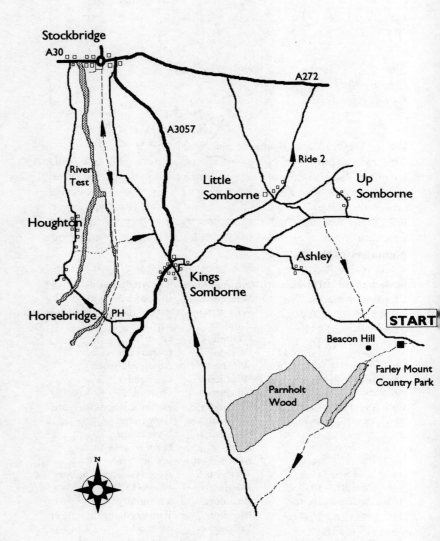

RIDE I

FARLEY MOUNT TO THE RIVER TEST

Short Route : 14 miles, 2½ hours
Long Route: 19 miles, 3 hours
Extended Route : 26 - 31 miles, 4 - 5 hours

Route Description

This ride provides a good balance of scenery (Beacon Hill, Parnholt Wood, River Test) with quiet country lanes and three bridleways, on downland to the west of Winchester. The route crosses the River Test via a footpath and it is well worth the one mile walk across the river and valley for the scenery. The old coaching town of Stockbridge provides an interesting stopping point for sightseeing.

The route offers three good bridleway sections. There is a superb descent through Parnholt Wood, which can be muddy and slippery in places. The route makes use of the old railway track to Stockbridge (now part of the Test Way) and this provides good off-road cycling with a flat and even surface. The final section back to Beacon Hill is on a bridleway with grassy surface and good views. The ride can be combined with Ride 2 to extend the total distance up to 31 miles.

There is a small Pub at Horsebridge (The John O'Gaunt) which can be recommended for its good beer and large portions of food. There are also pubs at Kings Somborne and Stockbridge. The River Test area provides a good location for a possible picnic.

Start   (OS Landranger sheet 185. Grid reference 407293)

From Winchester town centre, take the A3090 towards Romsey. Pass the Hospital to your left, and turn right at the next roundabout (B3041, signposted to Stockbridge A272). Almost immediately on your left is the road leading to Farley Mount (Sarum Road, not signposted). Take this road and at the crossroads go straight across and continue to the junction of the road to Hursley. Turn right, through Farley Mount Country Park to the Beacon Hill Car Park on the western fringe of Farley Mount (signposted Monument).

Stage 1   Beacon Hill to Kings Somborne

From the car park follow the track westwards, passing the monument. On reaching more open ground, continue to keep to the left towards the top of the ridge, until you reach the entrance to a wood. Take the left entrance into the wood (the other entrance, marked "Clarendon Way", should be ignored).

The descent through Parnholt Wood can become muddy in places and care should be taken on the steeper sections. Carry on down the track leaving Parnholt Wood to your right, and ignoring any right hand turns into the Forestry Commission land.

As you progress down the hill the surface improves. On reaching the metalled road at the bottom of the hill, turn right up a slight incline, and continue for about 3 miles until you reach Kings Somborne.

Stage 2   Kings Somborne and the Test Valley

At the junction with the main road in Kings Somborne, turn left (A3057 to Romsey). It is necessary to take this road only for a distance of ½ mile, then take a small road which forks on your right (signposted Horsebridge). Proceed to Horsebridge, where the John O'Gaunt pub is on your right.

Continue over the bridge on the road to Houghton. Just over the bridge on your right is a turn for the Test Way. If you do not wish walk by the River Test, you can take this route to Stockbridge.

The road to Houghton passes over several tributaries of the Test, past a mill and eventually over the Test itself. At Houghton Drayton, turn right opposite a garage, towards Houghton. Approximately ¼ mile from this junction there is a footpath to your right (signposted Clarendon Way). The entrance to this footpath is not obvious; it is on a left-hand bend, just before a bungalow.

About 100 yards down the footpath, you meet the River Test and this area makes a suitable resting or picnic place. Take the narrow wooden pedestrian bridge across the river and continue walking through the Test Valley for about 1 mile until Clarendon Way meets the junction with Test Way.

Long Route
At this point the Test Way follows the path of a disused railway. Turn left and cycle on the old railway track to Stockbridge, returning via the same route. This adds a total of 5 miles to your journey.

Stage 3   Return to Farley Mount
From the intersection, you now have to climb out of the Test Valley. Proceed up the hill ahead of you. At the top of the track, go ahead onto the metalled road and cycle along a ridge overlooking Kings Somborne. At the end of this ridge bear right and descend into Kings Somborne.

Cross diagonally over the A3057 and take the road ahead out of Kings Somborne, following signs for Little Somborne. After about a mile, where the road bears left, take the right turn towards Ashley. After about another mile bear left towards Up Somborne, ignoring the road ahead which leads into Ashley. A further mile on, an unmarked road joins from the left. (**Extended Route:** this is the connection with Ride 2. If you wish to combine these rides, turn left to Little Somborne and see page 16.)

Bear right with the road, and about 100 yards on is a bridleway to your right (unsignposted). Take this grassy track back towards Farley Mount. At the foot of Beacon Hill, where the bridleway meets a gravel track, turn right then immediately left and proceed to the road. At the road turn left and cycle up the hill back to the car park.

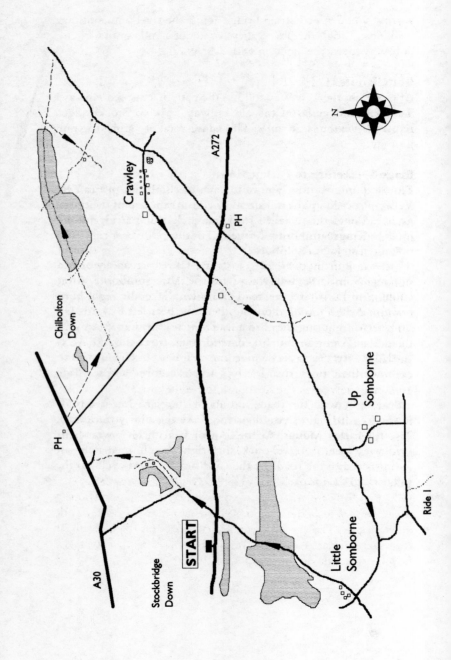

RIDE 2

STOCKBRIDGE AND CHILBOLTON DOWNS

Short Route: 12 miles, 2 hours
Extended Route: 26 – 31 miles, 4 – 5 hours

Route Description

This is quite a short route, with no hilly sections and can be recommended as a less energetic ride. For the more adventurous cyclist, this ride can also be combined with Ride 1 to extend the total distance up to 31 miles.

The village of Crawley, built as a model village at the turn of the century in mock-Tudor style is picturesque and worth a sightseeing trip. The bridleway section through the wood on Chilbolton Down is excellent. The surface is good and I have not found it get too muddy.

There is good access to the start point on the A272, but care should be taken when cycling the short distances down the A272 and A30 as traffic travels quite fast on these roads. From the car park there is pedestrian access to Stockbridge Down, which gives fine views over the surrounding countryside.

There are two pubs on the ride. The Leckford Hut can be recommended for its excellent food and friendly atmosphere. The Rack and Manger on the A272, which requires a slight detour to reach, also serves food.

Start   (OS Landranger sheet 185. Grid reference 388344)

Take the A272 from Winchester towards Stockbridge. About 7 miles from Winchester, just after a crossroads, there is a car park on the right. The car park is set back from the road, amongst trees and is for access to Stockbridge Down. Note that there is a height restriction on the entrance to this car park.

Stage 1   Stockbridge Down

From the car park, turn left down the A272 for a few hundred yards to the crossroads. Turn left down a narrow metalled road (unsignposted) and continue for about ½ mile until the road bears left. Ahead of you is a gate (signposted Bridleway). Go through this gate and continue up the road through park-like surroundings to a farm. At the farm continue straight ahead up a gravel track to the A30. Note that although this track is signposted as a bridleway from the A30, the gate may be padlocked, requiring you to lift your bike over. Turn right and cycle down the A30 for ½ mile to The Leckford Hut pub on your left.

Stage 2   Chilbolton Down and Crawley

Opposite The Leckford Hut, further along from a small road (signposted Crawley), is a bridleway (unsignposted). Turn down this grass track and proceed to a crossroads of tracks at the bottom. Continue straight ahead up a wide grassy track and bear left where a further track joins from the right. At the next crossroads of tracks, go straight ahead into the wood. Continue eastwards along the inside edge of the wood, ignoring any crossing tracks, until the track emerges into an open area. Turn right, and head south-westwards along the outside edge of the wood to the next crossroads, by a farm. Turn left and cycle to the road.

At the road, turn right and cycle downhill to a junction just before the pond at Crawley. For those wishing to detour to the Rack and Manger, continue straight ahead to the A272. Otherwise turn right into Crawley village.

Stage 3   Return via Little Somborne

Continue on the road through road through Crawley village to the junction with the A272. Directly across the road is a track (not immediately obvious due to the tree in the middle). Take this track, past farm buildings, to a junction with a metalled road. Turn right and cycle to Little Somborne. **(Extended Route:** just before Little Somborne as the road bears right, is a turn to your left. If you wish to combine this ride with Ride 1, take this left turn and see page 13.)

At the road junction on the outskirts of Little Somborne, turn right up a narrow metalled road back to the A272. At the main road, turn left and cycle the ½ mile along the A272 back to the car park.

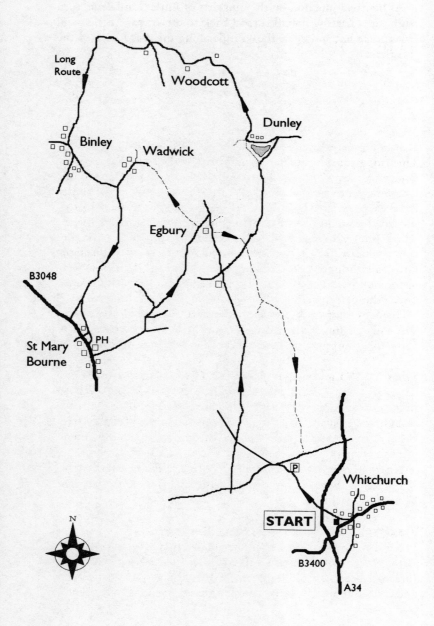

RIDE 3

THE BOURNE VALLEY

Short Route: 13 miles, 2 hours
Long Route: 17 miles, 2½ hours

Route Description

This ride provides an easy cycling trip around the picturesque Bourne Valley in North Hampshire. It is an ideal route for an introduction to riding off-road. A large proportion of the route is on country lanes, but they can be barely classified as roads. Indeed, I wouldn't want to drive my car down some of them! There is an excellent bridleway section on the last part of the ride. It has a firm gravel surface and winds its way through farmland, though it can become waterlogged for short distances in the hollows. There are no steep hills on the short route, and only a short steep uphill to Woodcott House on the long route.

There are shops and pubs near the start point in Whitchurch. The George Inn at the village centre in St Mary Bourne is a convenient stopping point and serves a good range of food.

Start   (OS Landranger Sheet 185. Grid reference 462481)

The start point for this ride is the small town of Whitchurch, 6 miles east of Andover. From Whitchurch centre, take the road to St Mary Bourne (Bell Street). About 200 yards along is a free car park to your left. Note there is a height restriction on entering this car park.

(Alternatively, if you continue to drive about a mile out of Whitchurch there is a large grass verge on your right, that can be used for parking).

Stage 1   Whitchurch to St Mary Bourne

From the car park turn left and cycle towards St Mary Bourne. After about 1½ miles you will come to a road junction where the road bears left. Take the second right turn (unsignposted) and after about ½ mile turn right at another crossroads (signposted Egbury). Cycle up this narrow metalled road for just over a mile, to another crossroads.

Short Route

At the crossroads continue straight on to Egbury. After ½ mile where the road goes down a hill, turn left. A short distance along, opposite Egbury Farm is a wide gravel track (unmade road leading to Wadwick). Turn right up this track and proceed up the incline, down a hill and bear left onto a metalled road at Wadwick. Continue on this road as you descend to St Mary Bourne. The road bears left leading you into the the centre of the village, next to The George Inn.

Long Route

At the crossroads, take a right turn (signposted Dunley). Continue for a mile until the road turns sharply right, just past Bradley Wood Farm. Take the track ahead of you and cycle downhill to meet the road again. Carry straight on downhill towards some houses, then bear left with the road and continue to Woodcott. At the staggered crossroads after Woodcott, turn right then left (signposted Binley). Pass the church, then cycle downhill to Binley. On entering Binley, bear left and turn next left up a short hill. At the T junction, turn right and descend to St Mary Bourne. The road bears left leading you into the the centre of the village, next to The George Inn.

Stage 2   Out of St Mary Bourne

Take the road the other side of The George Inn, turning back on yourself, to Egbury. After about 1 mile turn left to Egbury and continue to Egbury Farm. Just past Egbury Farm, turn right. At the top of the hill, a track forks to your left (signposted Bridleway). Follow this track through a field to the road. Turn right then take the next track to your left (unsignposted). Proceed downhill on the bridleway, round a "dogleg" and up a slope. At the top of the hill, take the left fork and continue on the track until the road.

Stage 3 Return to Whitchurch

Turn right and at the next road junction turn left . This is the road you cycled on out of Whitchurch. Proceed up the short hill and return to the car park.

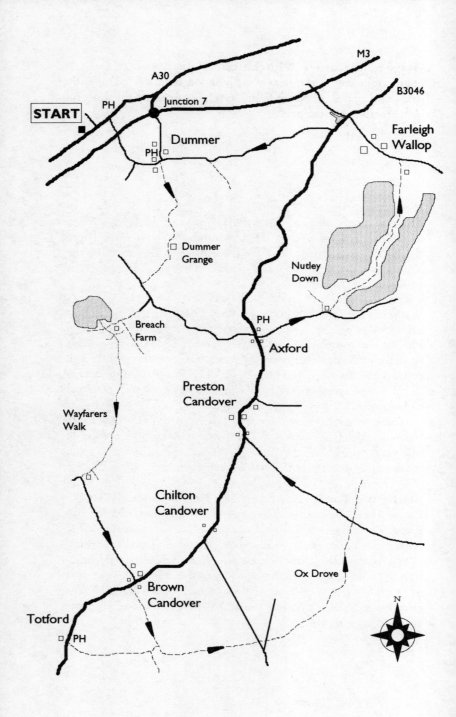

RIDE 4

THE WAYFARER'S WALK FROM DUMMER

Long Route: 19 miles, 3 hours

Route Description

This is a mainly off-road route for the more adventurous cyclist, in suprisingly open countryside just south of Basingstoke. There are good views across the North Hampshire downs from the Wayfarer's Walk, while in the woods on Nutley Down there is an abundance of wildlife.

The ride takes in 3 good bridleway sections; the Wayfarer's Walk, the Ox Drove, and Nutley Down. These sections can be a bit tricky in places, due to a slippery surface. There are no steep hills on the route and there are no particularly muddy sections since the chalk downs absorb the water well in wet weather. The route is mostly off road with some country lanes, though there is ½ mile of busy main road from the start point to reach the road to Dummer.

There is a good country pub at Axford (The Candover Crown), which serves a good range of beer and good food at reasonable prices. Alternatively by detouring to Totford, there is a similarly good pub (The Woolpack) earlier along the route.

Start   (OS Landranger Sheet 185. Grid reference 575462)

I have found difficulty in locating a good start point for this route. The village of Dummer consists of narrow lanes crowded with parked cars, and is best avoided. The most suitable parking is at a layby near Dummer, on the A30. From the M3 junction 7, proceed towards Basingstoke on the A30. Take the next left turn, shortly after the motorway junction (signposted Kings Worthy A33). Pass The Sun Inn and ½ mile further on is a large layby to your right.

Stage 1   The Wayfarer's Walk

From the layby, turn left onto the main road and head back towards The Sun Inn on a busy section of the A30. After ½ mile turn right up a minor road (signposted Dummer) and cycle into Dummer.

Just before the road junction in the centre of the village by the church, turn right along a concrete road between farm buildings (poorly signposted Right of Way in amongst the hedge). This is the Wayfarer's Walk and you may be able to check that you are on the path by spotting markers (black arrows on a white background). Pass through the farm buildings onto a gravel track, then continue following this track to Dummer Grange. Pass round by the Grange and follow the drive to a metalled road.

At the road, turn left and continue for ¼ mile before turning right up a road (signposted Breach Farm). Pass the farm and enter a wood. A few hundred yards on, where the track emerges from the wood, turn left. Proceed uphill between the hedgerows, over another track to the open down. Continue southwards over the down, alongside a field, then between hedges, for about 2 miles. Where the track becomes more defined, bear right by a house to a metalled road. Turn left and cycle to Brown Candover.

Stage 2   The Ox Drove

At the B3046, turn right. Take the next track about 100 yards on your left, by the telephone box (signposted Right of Way). Cycle up the incline, past the farm, until you come to a junction. Continue straight ahead, then bear left alongside a wood. (If you wish to detour to Totford, turn right and cycle 1 mile to the road where you will reach the Woolpack pub). Carry on the Ox Drove until you meet a road intersection. Proceed straight across both roads, onto the track ahead (signposted Right of Way). This may be muddy to start with, but soon becomes firmer. After about 2 miles this track meets another road. Turn left and cycle down to Preston Candover.

At the B3046 turn right and proceed to Axford. The ride continues along the road on your right in Axford (signposted Herriard). If you carry on a few hundred yards up the B3046, you will come across The Candover Crown pub.

Stage 3   Nutley Down

Take the right turn in Axford towards Herriard. Just less than a mile after the junction, there are 2 bridleways to your left. Take the second bridleway (the one after the house), to Nutley Down. Continue for 2 miles heading northwards on the main track through the wood until you reach a road. Turn left and cycle through Farleigh Wallop back to the B3046. At the crossroads, turn left onto the B3046, then take the next turn to your right (signposted Dummer). Follow this road into Dummer, and at the road junction in the centre of the village continue straight ahead. Bear right down to the A30 and turn left. Cycle the ½ mile back to the layby where you parked the car.

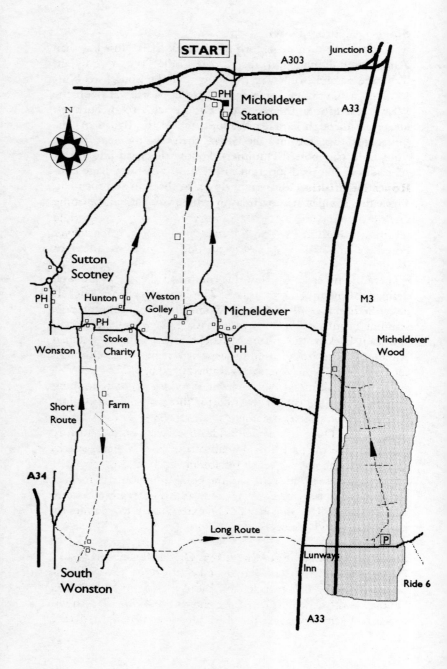

RIDE 5

MICHELDEVER

Short Route: 15 miles, 2 hours
Long Route: 19 miles, 2½ hours
Extended Route: 32 miles, 4½ hours

Route Description

This ride provides easy cycling on good tracks, taking in some fine open countryside and some pretty villages. The long route returns through the woodland that remains of Micheldever Forest, giving a good contrast to the open fields of the previous sections.

There are no steep hills on this route and the tracks are well defined, of mainly gravel surface. The bridleway from Micheldever Station is gently sloping downhill and passes through outstanding farmland. The long route has a good woodland section and leads back to the village of Micheldever, with its thatched cottages. There are no muddy sections on the route, although the track from Wonston can get waterlogged in places.

The Dever Arms at Micheldever provides a good stopping point towards the end of the ride for those on the long route. The pub serves food and there is also a general stores in the village. The Dove Inn at Micheldever Station is conveniently placed by the car park for the end of the ride. It serves snacks and is complete with a French restaurant.

Given the ease of this ride, and the good time you will make, I recommend opting for the long route as this gives a much more complete ride. This ride can also be extended up to 32 miles by joining up with Ride 6.

Start   (OS Landranger Sheet 185. Grid reference 518428)

From just south of Basingstoke, take the A303 towards Andover. Take the first turn left off the A303 (signposted Sutton Scotney and Micheldever). At the end of the slip road, turn left towards Micheldever. At the next junction turn right over a railway bridge, and follow the road alongside the railway to Micheldever Station. There is plenty of space to park in the British Rail car park.

Stage 1   From Micheldever Station

From the station car park turn right and cycle westwards past the recreation field. Just before the T junction at the top of the road, turn left down a gravel track (signposted Right of Way, but barely visible amongst the hedge). Continue for 2 miles down this track until you reach the metalled road at Weston Golley. Bear right and follow this road to a T junction. Turn right and cycle to Stoke Charity.

Continue through the village of Stoke Charity towards Wonston. Just before entering Wonston, the road bears right and there is a track ahead (unsignposted). Take this bridleway until it joins a narrow metalled road at a corner. Go straight ahead onto this road, through a farm (left bend then right bend) then up a track. This route is designated as a bridleway so there should be no problems with right of way through the farm.

Continue along the bridleway ignoring the left fork, which is the path of the old railway, until you meet the intersection of two tracks by some buildings.

Stage 2   Wonston
Short Route

Take a right turn (signposted Right of Way) and continue until you meet a road below the A34. Turn right along the road and about 100 yards further on turn right again (signposted Wonston). Note that traffic travels quite fast on this section of road, and it is possible to get to the Wonston road by walking the 100 yards on the path on the grass verge.

Cycle to Wonston, and at the junction turn right into the village. Turn almost immediately left and pass over the River Dever. Bear right and cycle parallel to the river for about a mile. Take a left turn (signposted Hunton) and proceed until you meet a more major road. Turn right and after about 1 ½ miles, turn right and return to Micheldever Station.

Long Route

Turn left and cycle in a straight line eastwards along a track (signposted Right of Way), until you come to a road at a corner. Go straight ahead onto the road and cycle to a T junction. Cross over the road to the track opposite (signposted Right of Way), and continue until you reach the A33. Cross the A33 to the road opposite (signposted Northington) and cycle under the M3 into Micheldever Forest. A few hundred yards on, turn left into the car park. **(Extended Route:** follow the instructions for Ride 6 short route from Stage 1. On your return, follow the directions through Micheldever Forest.)

Go through the car park to the gravel track ahead and turn right. The track bears to the left and goes downhill. Keep on this main track and ignore any turnings. After a mile this track ends in an intersection. Take the left fork and go under the M3 into the Forestry Commission area. Follow the metalled road round to the A33 by a gate. The gate may be locked so it will be necessary to lift your bike over the stile.

Turn left and cycle ½ mile up the main road then take a turn to your right (signposted Micheldever). As you enter the village, The Dever Arms is on your right. At the T junction turn left, leave the village and cycle alongside the railway line for 2½ miles until you come to a crossroads. Turn left and cross the railway line, then bear right and cycle on the other side of the line back to Micheldever Station.

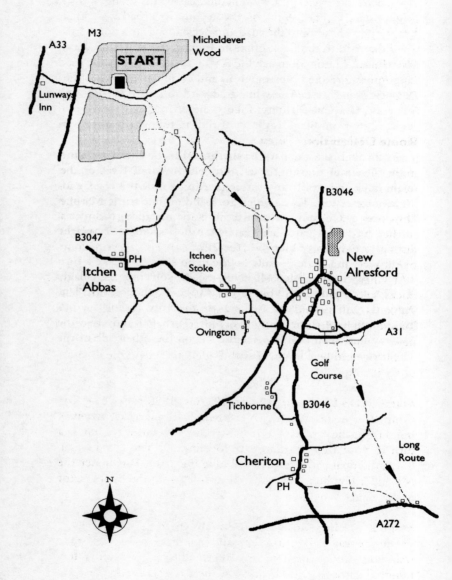

RIDE 6

ITCHEN STOKE DOWN

Short Route: 13 miles, 2 hours
Long Route: 20 miles, 3 hours
Extended Route: 33 – 38 miles, 5 – 6 hours

Route Description

This ride over downland to the north of Winchester, takes in the market town of Alresford with its tourist attractions such as the steam railway, as well as scenic routes along the river Itchen.

There are two good bridleway sections over Itchen Stoke Down on gravel and chalk surfaces. The long route includes a further bridleway to Cheriton that can be muddy in places during wet weather. There is a long country lane section along by the river Itchen that passes through a Ford.

At Cheriton there is a village green usually populated with ducks, and a pub (The Flower Pots) which serves snacks. The Public Bar of the pub is interesting since it has a well in the middle of the floor. The Plough Inn at Itchen Abbas serves a more extensive range of meals.

This ride can be combined with Ride 7 to extend the distance up to 38 miles.

Start   (OS Landranger Sheet 185. Grid reference 529363)

From Winchester, take the A33 towards Basingstoke. About 5 miles from the centre of Winchester, by The Lunways Inn, is a turn to your right (signposted Northington, The Candovers). Cross the dual carriageway, and take this road. Pass under the M3 and a few hundred yards on turn left into the car park for Micheldever Wood.

Stage 1   Itchen Stoke Down to Alresford

From the car park, turn left and continue down the road that you drove down in an easterly direction. After a few hundred yards the wood ends, and there is a track to your right (signposted Byway). Turn down this track and proceed straight on, ignoring tracks to your right. The surface improves, and just past a windmill take a left fork down a gravel track to a metalled road. Cross the road and continue on the track up to Itchen Stoke Down where 5 tracks intersect.

Take the track ahead of you, slightly offset to the left (signposted Footpath & Bridleway to Alresford). Continue down between the hedges, across a road, and over a stream to a junction of tracks. Bear left with the track to a road. At the road turn right and cycle to the B3046 between Old and New Alresford. Turn right and pass the pond, entering Alresford from Broad Street.

Stage 2   Cheriton
Short Route
From the top of Broad Street, turn right and cycle out of Alresford towards Winchester. As the road starts uphill take a right turn down the B3047 (signposted Kings Worthy). Now follow the directions from Stage 3.
Long Route
From the top of Broad Street, turn left (signposted Alton) and cycle to the outskirts of Alresford. Take the last turn on your right (Sun Lane) and continue until the road meets the A31 Alresford by-pass. Negotiating the by-pass is a bit tricky, but the safest way is to ignore the slip road to your left, turn right with the road and cross via the footbridge a little further down on your left. On the other side of the footbridge, turn left and cycle down between the fences to an entrance for the golf course. Ignore the bridleway to your right and carry on along the track for a few hundred yards to the next track on your right. Turn right here and cycle alongside the golf course. Keep along this track for a mile until you meet a metalled road.

Go straight ahead onto the road, and take the grassy track ahead of you (unsignposted). This track can be a bit wet to start with, but soon dries out as it reaches the top of the hill. There is now a good descent to main road by some houses. At the A272 turn right and a short distance along, where the road bends left, take another track to your right next to the bend chevron sign (unsignposted). Proceed along this track for about a mile ignoring any turns, until you come to a road. Turn right into the village of Cheriton. The Flower Pots pub is tucked away up a road to your left at the near end of the village. (**Extended Route:** Follow the directions from Stage 3 in Ride 7. You can choose either the short route to give a total distance of 33 miles, or the long route to give a total distance of 38 miles.)

Head northwards out of Cheriton along the B3046 towards Alresford. About ½ mile from Cheriton take a turn to your left (signposted Tichborne). Proceed through Tichborne, and under the Alresford by-pass to reach a junction. Take the road ahead of you, the B3047 (signposted Kings Worthy).

Stage 3   The Itchen valley

Pass over the river and continue uphill on the B3047. After about ½ mile take a left turn (unsignposted, except for a Ford sign). Cycle downhill, through the Ford and over a bridge. At the road junction turn right, and bear sharp left with the road into Ovington. Half way up the hill in the village, take a road to your right and cycle north-westwards above the river Itchen until you come to a T junction. Turn right and cross the river back to the B3047 at Itchen Abbas. Ahead of you is the Plough Inn.

At the junction, turn left and where the road bends left, take the narrow metalled road to your right (signposted School). At the crossroads bear right with the road and take the next track to your left, just passed a building (unsignposted). Cycle uphill until you join the track you cycled out on. Turn left then bear right, back to the road. Turn left and cycle back to the car park.

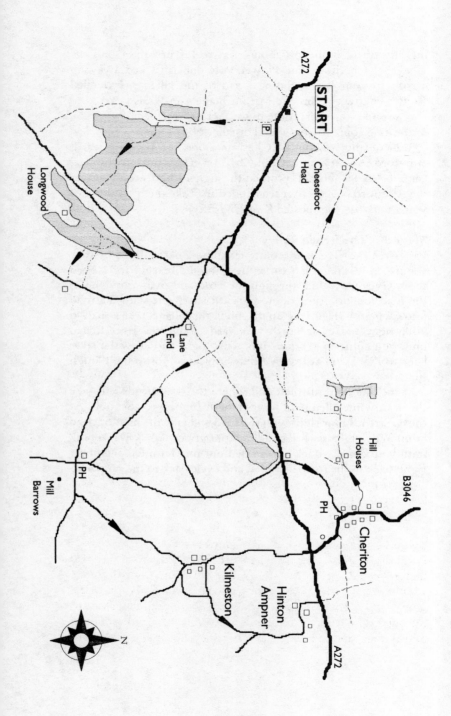

RIDE 7

CHEESEFOOT HEAD

Short Route: 13 miles, 2 hours
Long Route: 18 miles, 3 hours

Route Description

This route provides a leisurely ride around the start of the South Downs, to the west of Winchester. There is a good downhill from Cheesefoot Head, which ends in a sweeping track through woodland. In general the tracks are well defined and have a good surface, apart from a short section between Hill Houses and the South Downs Way extension. For those on the long route there is also a good downhill ride on narrow country lanes from Mill Barrows to Hinton Ampner. The climb back to Cheesefoot Head at the end of the ride, while not steep, can prove tiring.

There are 2 pubs on the route. "Millburys" at Mill Barrows serves a good choice of food as well as brewing their own beer. They have given a hospitable welcome to a group of muddy cyclists in the past! The Flower Pots at Cheriton serves snacks.

Start   (OS Landranger sheet 185. Grid ref 529278)

From Winchester, take the A31 towards Alton and after 2 miles take the A272 towards Petersfield. About 1 mile after the junction, towards the top of the hill, is a car park to your left. This can become quite full and there is now an additional car park a few hundred yards further on, on the right (note that this has a height restriction).

Stage 1   Descent from Cheesefoot Head

From the main car park, turn left on to the A272 and cycle a few hundred yards up to the top of the hill. Turn right into the additional car park, and take the gate ahead that leads you to the grassy track. Head southwards over the down until you come to the edge of a wood. Continue southwards on a more defined gravel track, and follow this as it bears left through the wood to a gate by a road. Turn left onto the road and cycle for about a mile until you leave the wooded area.

As the road bears left up a hill, there is a bridleway on your right (signposted Bridleway). This leads round the edge of a field, back on the direction you were heading, before re-entering the woods onto a grass track. The first part of this bridleway may not be well defined due to being ploughed. If you find this to be the case, it is easier to back-track down the road a few hundred yards and cut across to the track via a number of informal paths through the woods.

The path of the bridleway through the woods is marked by blue arrows. Head south-westwards for about ½ mile then take a left fork downhill. Cross over a gravel track and descend to a road. Turn left onto the road and cycle to a T junction. Go straight across to the track opposite (signposted Right of Way) and proceed along this for ½ mile until you encounter a junction of tracks.

Stage 2   Cheriton
Short Route
Continue ahead on the track, past a wood, to the A272. Turn right and cycle a few hundred yards on the main road until a minor road crosses. Turn left down this road (signposted Cheriton) and cycle to Cheriton. The Flower Pots pub is to your right as you enter the village.

Long Route
Turn along the track to your right to the road. Continue straight on at the road and cycle uphill to a T junction. Turn right and proceed to the crossroads at the top of the hill. Millburys is to your left. At the crossroads by Millburys, turn left then take the next turn to your left (signposted Kilmeston). This is a narrow metalled road that gives a fast downhill to a T junction at Kilmeston. Turn left (signposted Cheriton) and cycle through the village. At the end of the village, turn right opposite the telephone box down a narrow metalled road (unsignposted). Continue on this road through Hinton Ampner to the A272.

Cross the A272 to the narrow metalled road opposite (signposted Right Of Way). This soon gives way to a grassy track, and at the next junction of tracks turn left. This track leads you to the B3046 just to the south of Cheriton. Turn right along the B3046 into Cheriton. The Flower Pots pub is tucked away up a road to your left at the near end of the village.

Stage 3   Return to Cheesefoot Head

Continue northwards through Cheriton on the B3046 past the pond. Take the next turn to your left (signposted Hill Houses). Keep on the main track, past the houses, and downhill to a barn.

Surprisingly there is not really a satisfactory route from here to the South Downs Way extension. The most defined route is to turn left on the grassy track before the barn. This track can become very muddy, requiring you to walk. The track leads to a junction in a wooded area. Turn right along a narrow path that emerges from the wood then over a hill to a more defined track which is South Downs Way extension. Alternatively, if it is wet underfoot, you can reach the same point by a more difficult but drier route. Continue up the hill on the gravel track until it bends to the left. Take the narrow path ahead through the gate into the wood. The path emerges from the wood into a grass field via a gate. There is no discernable track here, but the course of the bridleway runs south-westwards across the field to the top left corner. Cross the field and turn left onto a track, then right at the next track. This is the South Downs Way extension.

Head north-westwards along the South Downs Way extension, over a road, then continue for a further mile. You will come to a junction of tracks by some buildings. Turn left and cycle up the gravel track to a gate. Go through to the narrow path that runs along by the fence, returning to the A272. Turn left and cycle back to the car park, 200 yards on your left.

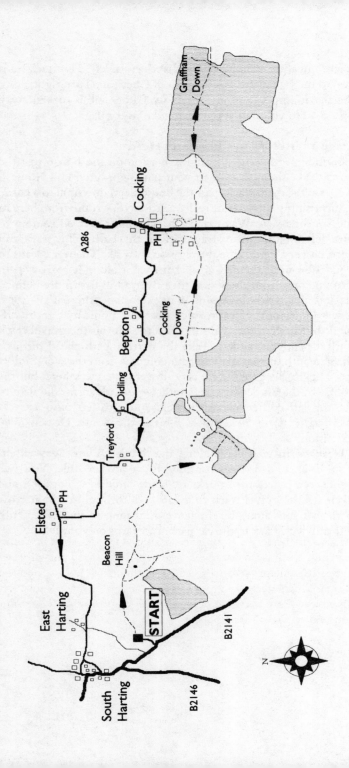

RIDE 8

THE SOUTH DOWNS

Short Route: 16 miles, 3 hours
Long Route: 22 miles, 4 hours

Route Description

This ride follows the popular South Downs Way on one of its most scenic portions, to the east of Petersfield. There are fine views from the chalk ridge over Harting and south to Chichester and the Isle of Wight.

The route is well signposted, both along the South Downs Way and the return leg along country lanes. The chalk track of the South Downs Way is well-defined, though it can be muddy through the wooded sections. The route is quite hilly with two short steep sections, and a steep hill back to the car park. There is an excellent long descent from Cocking Down, and for this reason I would not recommend cycling the route in the reverse direction.

The Three Horseshoes at Elsted is a typical country pub that serves good food and the garden has fine views of the South Downs along which you will have just cycled. The Potter and Vine pub at Cocking also serves food (sometimes limited to snacks).

Start   (OS Landranger Sheet 197. Grid reference 791181)

From the centre of Petersfield, take the A3 towards Portsmouth. At a roundabout at the bottom of the town, turn left (signposted B2146 Chichester). Continue on this road to a junction at South Harting. Turn right (signposted B2146 Emsworth) and proceed out of the village. At the bottom of a hill, turn left (signposted B2141 Chichester) and go uphill. At the top of the hill turn left down a narrow entrance between trees (signposted Viewpoint) and you will reach a car park.

Stage 1   Across the South Downs

From the car park, proceed eastwards over the grass area to a gate. Go through the gate and you will be confronted with two parallel tracks . The chalk track on your left is the South Downs Way, though you may find it easier to cycle up the hill on the grass track ahead of you. At the top of the hill, check that you are following the right track (signpost South Downs Way). Continue on the track over the summit and descend along a ridge overlooking East Harting to scrubland at the bottom, where there is a junction of tracks.

Here the South Downs Way takes a detour around Beacon Hill that lies ahead, although it is possible to go straight up the steep hill and rejoin the Way on the other side. Turn right (signposted South Downs Way) and follow round Beacon Hill through scrubland into a wooded area. Turn sharp left along a track to bring yourself back to the ridge on the other side of the hill. Bear right and proceed uphill, then descend along the ridge to a gate. Turn left along the farm track, then turn almost immediately right up a track towards a wood. On the other edge of the wood you will come to a junction of tracks. Turn left and pass some tumuli (Devil's Jumps), then enter another wooded area. Continue inside the wood, which can be muddy, and emerge to the ridge again.

The remainder of this stage is straightforward: The well-defined chalk track follows the ridge for 2 miles, without any steep hill sections. Descend from the top of Cocking Down through a farm to the A286.

Stage 2   Around Cocking

Cross the A286 to a track opposite and proceed up an incline to a farm (Hill Barn Farm, with notices for English Woodlands Timber) .

Short Route

At the farm, turn left by a barn down a muddy track (blank signpost). The track becomes less muddy and descends to a chalk pit. Take a right fork and another right to take you out of the chalk pit. The grassy track leads you to a road on the outskirts of Cocking. Turn left at the road, cross over a stream and proceed up to the A286. Turn left along the main road, and a short distance on your right is the Potter and Vine pub. Just before it, turn right down Bell Lane towards Bepton (unsignposted).

Long Route

This extension continues along the South Downs Way to Graffham Down before returning, thereby adding a further 6 miles to your trip.

Proceed through the farm on the South Downs Way up the long ascent ahead. Go through a gate and continue uphill with the woods to your right. At the top of the hill, enter the woodland and keep on the main track. Note that this section of the ride can be rather muddy at times. Continue for 2 miles and emerge from the woods at a junction of tracks. From here there are good views eastwards to the River Arun. Turn round and cycle back on the same route back to Hill Barn Farm. At the farm, turn right by a barn down a muddy track (blank signpost) and follow the Short Route directions to Cocking village.

Stage 3   Return from Cocking

This stage of the route follows country lanes back beneath the ridge that you cycled along. The junctions are well signposted and provided you follow signs for Harting, you should not have any difficulty in finding the route.

Continue on the road from Cocking to Bepton. At Bepton proceed straight ahead to Didling. At the road junction at Didling, turn left towards the downs (signposted Treyford, Harting) then bear right with the road and continue to Treyford. Just passed Treyford where the road goes uphill, turn left (signposted Elsted, Harting) and continue to a T junction at Elsted. The Three Horshoes pub is a short distance down the road to your right. Turn left at the junction and cycle through East Harting to South Harting. Bear left with the road into the village centre.

The route now follows the road you drove along to the start point, up the steep hill. Cycle out of the village on the B2146. At the bottom of a hill, turn left (signposted B2141 Chichester) and proceed up the steep hill section. At the top of the hill turn left back down the narrow entrance between trees (signposted Viewpoint) to return to the car park.

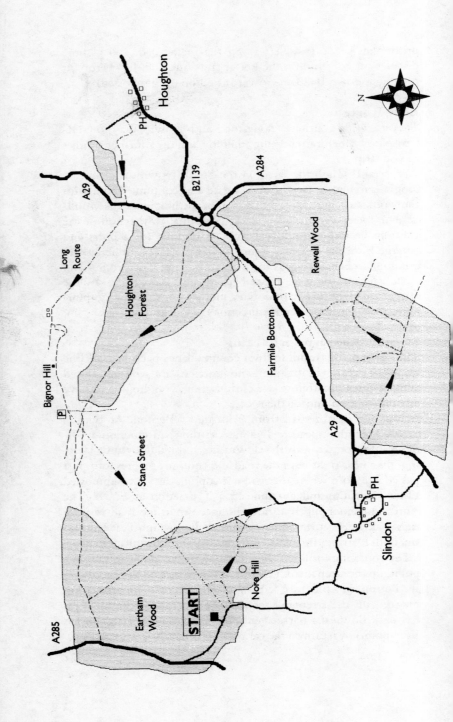

RIDE 9

STANE STREET

Short Route: 12 miles, 2 hours
Long Route: 17 miles, 3 hours

Route Description

This is a ride around woodland to the east of Chichester on the edge of the South Downs. Eartham Wood is riddled with bridleways and is worth cycling around in its own right. From Bignor Hill there are fine views; on a clear day you can look across Bognor and Selsey Bill to the sea.

The ride is on well-defined tracks, though route-finding through Rewell Wood is a little difficult. There is one uphill section on the ride, the ascent to Bignor Hill. On the short route, this is a long but gentle climb through Houghton Forest. The long route uses one of the less strenuous sections of the South Downs Way, but there are still two steep climbs. The last section of the ride returns down the path of the old Roman road of Stane Street that ran from London to Chichester.

There are two possible places to obtain refreshment. The cafe at Fairmile Bottom is a convenient stopping point for both routes, though it can get busy in summer. The George and Dragon at Houghton is a well-furnished pub that serves interesting meals.

Start   (OS Landranger Sheet 197. Grid reference 938107)

From Chichester, take the A27 towards Brighton, then turn left along the A285 towards Petworth. About 4 miles from the junction turn right, back on yourself, down a minor road (signposted Bognor). About ½ mile down this road on your left is the gravel entrance to the car park at Eartham Wood.

Stage 1   Eartham and Rewell Woods

Cycle out of the car park back to the road and turn left. After a few hundred yards, where the road bends to the right, turn left in between houses (signposted Bridleway, North Wood). Cycle into the wood then at the bottom of a dip, take the right fork. This rough track runs south-eastwards slightly uphill, at the foot of Nore Hill. At the junction of tracks turn left and cycle downhill to the T junction at the edge of the woods. Turn right onto the gravel track and keep heading south-eastwards as the surface becomes tarmaced. At the T junction half-way up a short hill, turn left and cycle into Slindon. As the road bears right, turn left up a narrow road and follow this to the junction with the A29.

Cross the A29 to the track opposite, slightly to your right (signposted Public Bridleway). Go down this track into the woods and keep on the main track for 3/4 mile until you come to some earthworks. The track you are on goes ahead out of the woods, through a gate. However the track you require is hidden to your left, made all the more difficult by the signpost being broken. This track is up the bank to your left and can be distinguished by the single bar gate. Head north-eastwards uphill, ignoring any turnings, continuing eastwards with the track at the top of the hill.

You will come to a junction of tracks, this time with a signpost. Turn left (signposted Public Bridleway) and proceed down a steep downhill. The track leaves the woods and emerges to a grass area above the A29. In order to avoid cycling along this horrendous road, turn right along a grass track situated about halfway between the wood and the road. Where the track re-enters the wood, take a left fork and descend to a layby on the A29.

Cross the road and cycle north-eastwards on the A29 for 300 yards until you are opposite Fairmile Bottom Cafe. Turn left off the road down a grassy track (signposted Public Bridleway). After a short distance this turns right and runs parallel to the road. It may be slightly overgrown in places, but is preferable to the main road. After ½ mile the track enters a wood and bears left onto a more defined track. Follow this track until it leads out of the wood onto a narrow road.

Stage 2   To Bignor Hill
Short Route
Cross the road to the track opposite and continue heading north-westwards uphill for 3/4 mile. Here the route joins a more major gravel track heading in the same direction. Keep heading north-westwards as the track continues slightly uphill for just over a mile to a junction of tracks. Conveniently, there is a bench at this intersection! Turn right and cycle due North for a short distance to the car park at Bignor Hill.

Long Route
Turn right and cycle down to the A29, joining by a round-about. Head diagonally across the roundabout to the B2139 and descend down the steep hill to Houghton. The George and Dragon is on your left as you enter the village. Take the next left turn after the pub and pass by a white thatched cottage. A few hundred yards down this road turn left up a gravel and chalk track that winds between the fields (unsignposted). You are now on the South Downs Way and behind you as you climb are fine views of the River Arun. The track runs alongside a wooded area before coming to the A29. Turn right and cycle a few hundred yards along the main road, then turn left onto a chalk track.

Follow the main track as it bears north-westwards, then de-scends to some black barns. Just beyond the barns is a track to your left that is obscured by a hedge. Turn left up this track and bear immediately right, then climb to Bignor Hill. Go through the gate to the summit marked by a memorial stone, then bear westwards to the car park. This is a fast descent on a good surface, but be careful of walkers.

Stage 3   Return along Stane Street
From the car park at Bignor Hill, go through the barrier in the south corner. There are a number of tracks here and the way can be confusing. Leave the South Downs Way which heads westwards up to the radio masts, and proceed south-westwards on one of the tracks across the scrubland. The tracks shortly converge and lead to a gate. Go through the gate and cycle alongside the fence to the next junction of tracks. Fortunately there is now a signpost (Stane Street) that allows you to check that you are on the right route.

The path of Stane Street now runs south-westwards in a straight line back to Eartham Wood. It passes through a field, where it is not clearly defined, up a farm track, then along a tree-lined embankment that has some rather awkward exposed roots. On entering Eartham Wood the surface improves to a gravel track which leads back to the road. Turn right and a few hundred yards on your right is the car park.

RIDE 10

THE NEW FOREST: BOLDERWOOD

Short Route: 15 miles, 2 -- 3 hours

General points about cycling in the New Forest

The New Forest provides a large area for off-road cycling across heaths and through woodland in outstanding surroundings. There are a number of differences to cycling in the New Forest as compared to other rides in this book, and these are worth emphasising.

There are no rights of way in the New Forest such as those offered by the bridleway system. Cycling access has recently been restricted, so that you are now only allowed to cycle on the gravelled tracks. You may have spotted the somewhat ambiguous notices stating "Cycling on Forest Roads only" as well as no cycling markers on grass tracks leading from car parks. The New Forest Forestry Commission produce a small leaflet (available from Tourist Information offices free of charge) that lays down a cycling code. Regarding access, it states that you should keep to the gravelled "Forest Roads" (i.e. gravel tracks) and that cycling on grass rides and unmade tracks is not permitted. It also states that you should give way to walkers and horse riders, travel at moderate speed and approach ponies and cattle with caution. That said, there are still enjoyable rides to be had in the New Forest, and the two rides I have chosen in this area pass through some of the best scenery while adhering to these restrictions.

Getting lost seems to be part of cycling in the Forest, but I have found that using a compass for navigating is the most reliable means of finding the right route. Consequently the directions given for these rides refer to points of the compass. The maps that I have drawn for Rides 10 and 11 may not be sufficient for your needs. If you manage to stay on the described route then they will provide enough information, but if

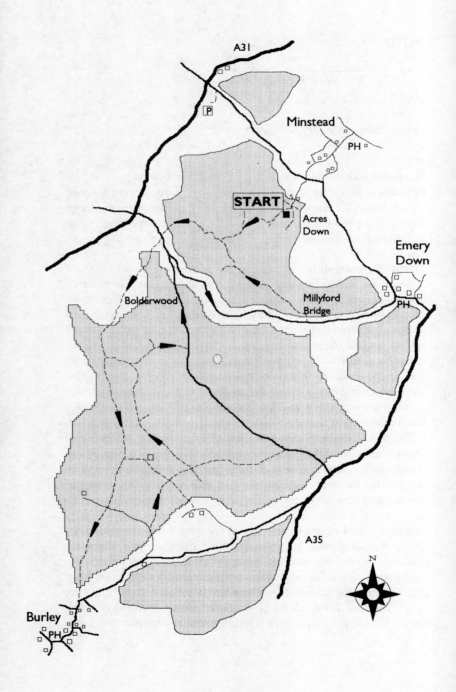

A31

P

Minstead

PH

START

Acres
Down

Emery
Down

PH

Bolderwood

Millyford
Bridge

A35

N

Burley

PH

you become lost then you may need detail of a broader area. If you are going to do either of these rides, then I would strongly advise you to buy an Ordnance Survey map of the area. (OS Landranger map No. 195 covers both rides and the OS also produce an Outdoor Leisure map for the New Forest).

The New Forest becomes very busy in summer, so I have chosen two rides away from the more popular area, with easier access to the start point. Nevertheless you may find traffic jams at M27 Junction 1. There is a blanket 40 mph speed limit in the Forest which should be adhered to. In many cases this is too fast and you should slow down when passing animals.

In general, pubs in the New Forest offer a poor service. They are frequently shut, and a lot do not serve food. Where there is a pub near to the route, I have mentioned this.

Route Description

This ride is through wooded inclosures that are typical of New Forest scenery. It follows a route through woods around Bolderwood, where there is a deer sanctuary, to Burley. The return leg from Millyford Bridge follows alongside a stream and is particularly scenic.

The start point for this ride is from one of the more accessible points in the Forest. However, in comparison with some of the better known locations in the region, it is suprisingly quiet. The route gives an easy ride on firm gravel tracks, making it suitable for cycling in wet weather.

There are two pubs near to the ride. The Queens Head at Burley is a busy pub that serves a good choice of food. The New Forest Inn at Emery Down also serves food. There is a good picnic spot at Millyford Bridge and a Cafe at Acres Down that serves enormous helpings of home-made cakes.

Start   (OS Landranger Sheet 195. Grid reference 268097)

From Southampton take the M27 westwards, and pass junction 1 onto the A31 towards Ringwood. Go up a hill and pass signs to Stoney Cross. At the top of the hill, about 2 miles from the end of the M27, turn left (signposted Emery Down). Continue on this road for just over a mile until a minor road intersects. Turn right down the narrow lane (unsignposted, the

49

left turn is signposted Newtown, Minstead) and proceed to the end of the road, where 4 tracks originate. Take the second from right fork and a few hundred yards on turn left into Acres Down car park. Note that when returning home, it is not possible to turn right onto the A31.

Stage 1   To Burley through Bolderwood

From the car park, turn left onto the gravel track and head south-westwards. Go through a gate and follow the main track downhill. Where a track joins from the left, bear right over a stream to head north-westwards. Keep following the main track as it bears left uphill and through a gate to emerge from the wood into a small car park (unmarked).

Cross diagonally over the metalled road and take the track ahead of you in a southerly direction. This is a fast downhill section on a well defined gravel track. Pass the Deer Sanctuary sign and cross over a stream, staying on the main track. Proceed uphill and continue south-west, over a narrow metalled road, until you reach the end of the wood. You are now on the outskirts of Burley. A mile further down the road to your right is The Queens Head, located in the centre of Burley.

Stage 2   To Millyford Bridge

Turn left along the metalled road and cycle north-eastwards for about a mile until you reach a house on your right. Take a left turn opposite (signposted Old House) into the wood. Fork right onto the gravel track (the road is private) and go through a gate into the inclosure. Proceed north, then north-eastwards on the track until you cross over a stream and go uphill. Towards the top of the hill, turn left along another gravel track. Continue on this track for a mile then where it bears left, turn right onto another track. (Note that if you reach a building to your right, you have turned left too soon). Proceed uphill and bear right to reach a road (Bolderwood Ornamental Drive).

Turn left and cycle on the road, past the busy car park at Bolderwood, to a junction with another road. Turn right and cycle south-eastwards for just over 2 miles on this road, then turn left into the car park at Millyford Bridge. (1 mile further down the road at Emery Down is the New Forest Inn). There is an open grassy area here that is ideal for picnics.

Stage 3   Return from Millyford Bridge
From Millyford Bridge car park, take a gravel track in a northerly direction into the wood and across the stream. Bear north-west with the track and go through a gate into the wood. Continue north-west on the track until you reach a left bend down a hill. Fork right onto another track and proceed to a junction. Turn right onto this track and take the right fork up a hill. This is the track you cycled out from Acres Down on. Go through the gate and cycle back to the car park.

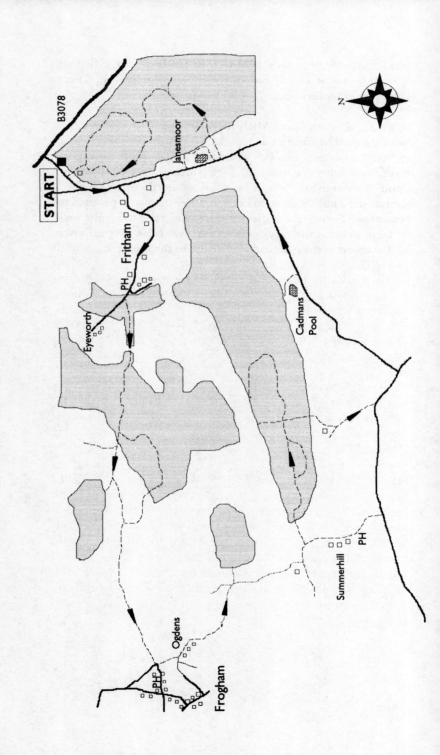

RIDE 11

THE NEW FOREST: FRITHAM

Short Route: 15 miles, 2½ – 3 hours

Route Description

Please refer to the general points regarding cycling in the New Forest, given in Ride 10. This route gives a more diverse ride, taking in open heathland on the edge of the New Forest as well as the more expected wooded inclosures. There is a superb downhill section through Fritham Wood and over the heathland to Frogham. Due to the restrictions on cycling access, this ride involves a short walk over part of the heath, which can be muddy in wet weather.

As with Ride 10, I have chosen an easily accessible start point. This results in a short ride along minor roads to begin with, but this does have the benefit of clear directions for the start of your ride.

There are two pubs near to the ride: The High Corner Inn at Summerhill is a popular pub that serves a good choice of food, and The Foresters Arms at Frogham also serves food. In addition there are plenty of suitable picnic spots on this ride, particularly Cadmans Pool.

Start   (OS Landranger Sheet 195. Grid reference 248150)

From Southampton take the M27 westwards and exit at Junction 1. Turn right on the roundabout below the motorway (signposted B3079 Landford). (Note that this might be congested with traffic, but that most will be turning left to Lyndhurst). About a mile further on take a left fork (signposted B3078 Fordingbridge) and continue for another 2 miles, then turn left down a narrow metalled road (signposted Fritham). Almost immediately to your left is the car park (marked Longcross).

Stage 1   To Fritham and Frogham

From the car park turn left and cycle south-westwards along the road. Bear left with the road and take a right turn a little further on (signposted Fritham and Eyeworth Only). Proceed westwards through Fritham until you reach the Royal Oak pub. Take the right hand fork (north-west) and turn left into the car park amongst the trees (marked Fritham).

Take the track nearest to the road, on your right as you enter the car park. Go westwards downhill through the wood, keeping on the main gravel track until you reach a bridge (Fritham Bridge). Bear right, then left, then right again on the main track. Head westwards on the main track, until you emerge from the wood to a heath. Continue westwards until the track forks. Take the left hand fork and cycle south-westwards along the track, at the top of a ridge. At the next fork take the right hand track, keeping westwards along the ridge. From the top of the ridge, descend south-westwards with the track until you meet a road. (Ahead of you, ½ mile along the road is The Foresters Arms at Frogham).

Stage 2   Frogham to Cadmans Pool

At the junction with the road turn left down another track in a south-easterly direction. You will reach a stream which you can either cycle through or cross via the footbridge, into Ogdens car park. Proceed out of the car park and where the track bears right, turn left and cycle alongside some houses. The track ends after ½ mile and you should take a more grassy path through a barrier in a south-easterly direction. When you come to an open area in front of a wood, turn right. You will have to dismount here and walk the next ½ mile across the sandy heath, due to the cycling restrictions. Walk southwards over the hill top on a sandy path. From here there is no single defined path, but you should follow the paths in a south to south-easterly across the scrub. Note that this can be muddy for a short distance. After ½ mile you will reach a stream which you can cross via the footbridge.

On the other side of the stream, turn left and cycle north-east along the gravel track. Where this bends to the right, turn left into Woodford Bottom car park. (½ mile further up the track you have turned off is the High Corner Inn at Summerhill). At the far end of the car park take a gravel track in a north-easterly direction into the wood. Continue north-east along this track through the wood for about a mile until a more major track crosses. Turn right onto this track and proceed out of the inclosure. Pass some buildings and continue to the road. Bear left onto the road and a short distance further on turn left down another road (signposted Fritham). Head north-eastwards on this flat and straight road for 2½ miles to a T junction. Halfway along this road, to your left is Cadmans Pool which makes a good picnic spot.

Stage 3   Return via Janesmoor

At the T junction, turn left and just before Janesmoor Pond car park, take a track to your right into the wood. (Note that you can return to the start point by continuing along the road). Proceed eastwards along the gravel track then bear right and cycle in a left hand arc until you come to a right hand bend at the bottom of a hill. Turn left and emerge from the inclosure through the gate ahead. Cross the open grassland on the gravel track and enter another inclosure opposite, via another gate. Go westwards for a short distance inside this wood until you meet another track. Bear left and cycle north-westwards uphill for a mile until you reach the road at a Forestry works. Turn right along the road back to the car park, a short distance on your right.

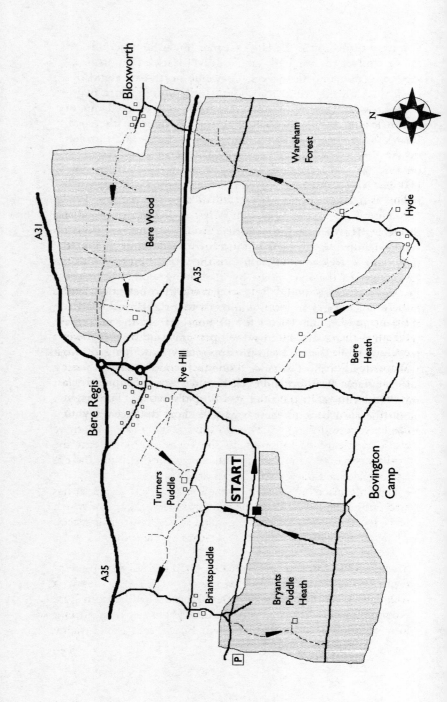

RIDE 12

THE DORSET HEATHLANDS

Short Route: 13 miles, 2½ hours
Long Route: 17 miles, 3 hours

Route Description

This is a route around the heathlands to the west of Poole, taking in a section of Wareham Forest. It is a superb woodland ride, with two excellent sections through attractive woods on good paths. There are a number of tourist attractions in the immediate area for those who wish to combine these with the cycling.

The tracks used on this ride are generally well defined, and as there are only two short uphills, from Bere Regis and from Briantspuddle, this makes for easy cycling. The grass tracks through the woodland sections make particularly enjoyable cycling, while there is also a more expected gravel track through Wareham Forest. There are two excellent downhills passing through the heathland on gravel and sand tracks on the last section of the ride. The ride holds up suprisingly well in wet weather, though there are a couple of places in Bere Wood that can become waterlogged. Though this is a fairly easy ride, there are a couple of tricky parts on the route: At one point the bridleway passes through a sawmill, and at another point there is a poorly defined track across a grass field.

The only place on the route is the town of Bere Regis. It has two pubs (The Royal Oak and the Drax Arms), both of which serve food. There are also two general stores in the main street. There are plenty of places for picnic stops on the route.

Start   (OS Landranger sheet 194. Grid ref 825924)

From Poole take the A35 westwards until you reach a roundabout on the outskirts of Bere Regis. Turn left into Bere Regis and follow the road round to the left rather than turning into the town centre (signposted Bovington, street name

Southbrook). Continue on this road for 2½ miles until a crossroads. Turn right (signposted Bovington Camp) and pass the entrance to the Tank Museum. Take the next turn to your right (signposted Waddock Cross) and continue for a mile to a crossroads. On your right is a small parking area. (If this is full, there is larger car park 1 mile down the road to your left at Cull-peppers Dish).

Stage 1   River Piddle and Wareham Forest

From the crossroads take the right hand road in an easterly direction (signposted Bere Regis). Cross over the river then where a road joins from the left, turn right onto a gravel track (unsignposted). Proceed on the track until it meets a road. Turn right onto the road and after ½ mile turn along a track to your left, before the electricity pylon (unsignposted). Continue past a number of houses, with the river Piddle to your left, until the track ends in a grass area before a house. Take the narrow path in the right hand corner ahead and enter the woods. Cross the stream and follow the main path south-eastwards through the woods (occasionally signposted with blue arrow markers). Emerge from the woods and follow the path alongside a fence by a riding school to reach a sawmill. The route of the bridleway runs along the right hand edge of the sawmill and through the bridle gate at the entrance to the road. This may be tricky to navigate due to piled logs.

Turn left onto the road, cross over the river and cycle for a mile until you reach a sharp left bend by Bere Lodge. Go straight ahead onto the gravel track into Wareham Forest. Follow the main track north-eastwards through the forest until you reach a road. Cross over the road and enter the woods opposite. Where the main track bears right, fork left up a path (blue arrow marker) and proceed to a main road. Cross the A35 to the minor road opposite (signposted Bloxworth) and cycle to Bloxworth.

At the T junction in the centre of the village, turn left and keep ahead down a no through road. At the end of this road, go through the metal gate into the grass field (blue arrow marker, broken bridleway sign). Follow round the right hand edge of the field, then cross the field to a metal bridle gate into the woods. There is only a faintly discernable path through the grass, but by locating the metal gate you can find the route. Once inside the wood, the way is more defined. Head westwards on the grass path, crossing a number of gravel tracks, following the blue arrow markers. After about a mile, you will reach a junction at the bend of a gravel track. Turn left up the grass track (blue arrow marker) and go up the short incline to a ridge. From here there are superb views across Wareham Forest to the Purbeck Hills. Continue on this grass track until it reaches a gravel track, then turn left and descend to a road. Turn right onto the road and go down the steep hill to the outskirts of Bere Regis. Cross over the main road, go through the gate opposite, then take the next left turn down the old road into Bere Regis.

Stage 2   Turners Puddle
Leave Bere Regis on the road south towards Bovington (signposted Bovington, street name Southbrook). Proceed up Rye Hill and at the top turn right down a gravel track (Camping signpost). Pass the campsite and go through a gate, then up a short hill. At the top of the hill, bear right then left onto a ridge alongside a gravel pit. Where the next track crosses, turn left onto a good downhill section. Beware that this ends in soft sand just before a farm. Turn left to avoid the farm and proceed to a road. At the road, turn right and a short distance further the road ends at a church.

Stage 3   Bryants Puddle Heath
Short Route
Turn left down a track and cross the river Piddle via a ford. Continue on the semi-metalled track to a road. Turn left onto the road and cycle uphill to the crossroads where you parked the car.
Long Route
Continue ahead passing the church onto a gravel track (signposted Bridleway to Moor Lane). Keep on this track, following the course of the river until you reach a road.

Turn left and proceed through Briantspuddle, then uphill to a road junction. Take the right fork as you approach the junction, then continue across the road to a track opposite (blue arrow marker). Go into the wood on another good downhill section, following the blue arrow markers. Where the track enters a more densely wooded area bear left, then a little further on bear right onto a well-defined track and continue to a road. Turn left onto the road, then about a mile further on take a left turn (signposted Waddock Cross). Follow this road back to the crossroads where you parked the car.

THE PURBECK HILLS

Short Route: 14 miles, 2½ hours
Long Route: 21 miles, 4 hours

Route Description

This is a ride along the ridge of the Purbeck Hills, a popular off-road cycling area. The ride leads to the superb sandy beach at Studland, and is best appreciated on a clear day when you can get the benefit of the fine views from the Purbeck Hills. There are particularly superb views of Poole Harbour and Swanage Bay from Nine Barrow Down. Both routes pass through the historic village of Corfe, by the ruins of its Norman Castle.

The ride is a mixture of gravel tracks and grass paths. Crossing the Purbecks from west to east gives three good steep descents. This results in a long climb from Corfe to Ailwood Down, but at least this incline can be cycled. There is an easier return through heathland on the edge of Poole Harbour.

The Isle of Purbeck is a busy place during the summer season, and traffic jams are commonplace. Since this is really a ride for the more experienced cyclist, I have based the ride on a distance of 21 miles, chosing one of the more easily accessible points to start from. The ride can be shortened to 14 miles, but be prepared that the start point for this route can be congested in summer. An alternative for those living in the Bournemouth and Poole areas is to take their bike across on the Studland Ferry.

There are plenty of options to stop for refreshment on the route. Corfe has a number of pubs (The Bankes Arms Hotel offers a range of meals) as well as a stores and bakery. A quieter location is The Bankes Arms at Studland, which serves snacks. There is also also a cafe at Knoll Beach that includes a selection of home-made cakes.

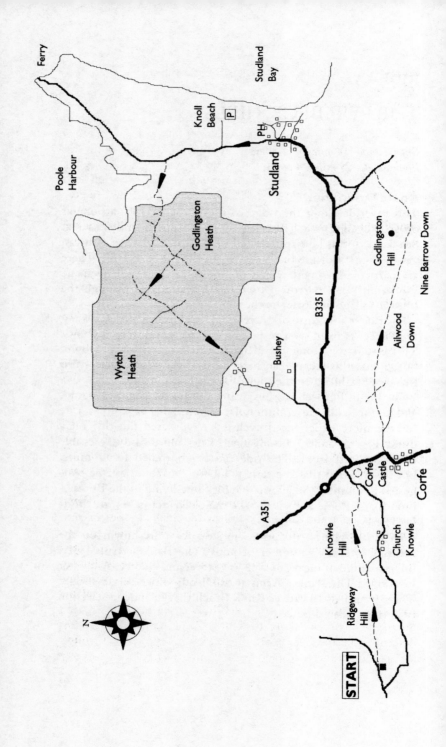

Start   Long Route   (OS Landranger sheet 195. Grid reference 905817)

From Poole take the A35 then the A351 westwards to Wareham. Follow the Wareham bypass towards Swanage and after crossing the River Frome, take the next right turn (signposted Creech, Steeple, Kimmeridge). Continue along this road for 2 miles, when you will begin to climb up to the ridge. Immediately on passing through the white gate, turn left into the car park (signposted Steeple Picnic Area). Note that the car park is just inside the army firing range area and could conceivably be closed, though this is most unlikely since the main ranges are further to the west. Follow the directions commencing at Stage 1.

Start   Short Route: (OS Landranger sheet 195. Grid reference 033835)

From Poole take the A35 then the A351 westwards to Wareham. Follow the A351 past Wareham to Corfe and turn left opposite the castle along the B3351 to Studland. Continue through Studland following signs for the Studland Ferry and ½ mile further on turn right into Knoll Beach car park. For this route you will need to follow the directions commencing at Stage 3.

Stage 1   Ridgeway and Knowle Hills (Long Route only)

From Steeple picnic area take the track at the east end of the car park (signposted Corfe Castle 3½). Head eastwards up the track between hedgerows as it ascends to Ridgeway Hill. From here there are superb views over Kimmeridge to the sea. Continue eastwards along the ridge then follow the track as it descends to a metalled road. Go through the gate, along the road for 100 yards, then through the gate ahead onto the track (signposted Ridge Path Corfe Castle). Head eastwards up the incline to Knowle Hill. Here the track runs out into a grass path. Continue eastwards along the ridge path, through some gates, until the path reaches the edge of the ridge by a stone marker. Proceed down the chalk track towards Corfe Castle. Unfortunately this descent is marred by some rather awkward gates. Go through the gate onto the road below the castle, turn left and cycle to the junction with the A351. Turn right along the A351 into Corfe.

Stage 2   Nine Barrow Down

As you go up the hill into Corfe take the turn to your left that leads under the railway bridge (unsignposted). A short distance along, take the bridleway to your left (signposted Ulwell 3 3/4). Climb up alongside the ridge until you come to a junction with a track. Go straight ahead through the gate, towards the radio mast (signposted Ridge Path). Head eastwards on the grass track as it continues to climb, until you reach another gate. From here there are fine views over Poole Harbour to your left. Go through the gate and cycle on the ridge for nearly two miles along Ailwood and Nine Barrow Downs. Just below Godlingston Hill, bear right onto a rough chalk track. Follow this track down a steep descent until you reach a road.

Turn left onto the road, then a few hundred yards on fork to the right (signposted Studland Ferry). Proceed to the junction with the B3351, then turn right and cycle into Studland. The Bankes Arms is on a minor road to your right, leading to the beach. Continue on the main road through Studland towards the ferry. After ½ mile you will reach Knoll Beach car park, to your right.

Stage 3   Knoll Beach to Corfe

From Knoll Beach proceed on the road towards Studland Ferry. Nearly a mile from the car park, where the road bears right, turn left down a sandy track by a bus stop (unsignposted apart from a small National Trust sign marking Godlingston Heath). You will shortly come to a white single bar gate that marks the National Trust boundary and from here on the bridleways are designated with blue arrows. Continue on the track until it crosses a stream, then fork immediately left (blue arrow). This track becomes wide and road-like, so after ½ mile you should look for a minor gravel track that crosses. Turn right and go over the single bar gate into the wood (blue arrow). Where this track bears left, continue straight ahead on the minor sandy track to the edge of the wood. Go through the field ahead via the 2 gates (blue arrow), then turn left onto the gravel track. Head south-westwards on this track until you reach a junction. Cross over the road and continue south-westwards through the woods for a further mile. At the edge of the woods, go through the gate onto a road, through a farm, then bear left and cycle to a junction with another road. Continue straight ahead to the B3351 and turn right. Beware that this section of road may be blocked by a traffic jam. Proceed to the junction of the B3351 with the A351, opposite Corfe Castle.

Stage 4   Return to Steeple (Long Route only)

The route back to the car park is to retrace the outward leg of Stage 1 along Knowle and Ridgeway Hills. As an easier alternative, you can follow the road at the bottom of the ridge, through Church Knowle and Steeple, back to the car park. This road is relatively flat, apart from the short but steep uphill to the car park.

Turn right onto the A351 then almost immediately left alongside the castle (signposted Church Knowle). After passing the castle, take the bridleway to your right (signposted Knoll Hill) and climb to the ridge via those awkward gates. Cycle westwards along the top of the ridge then descend to the narrow road. Take the track ahead leading up the hill (signposted Ridgeway Hill) and continue back to the car park.

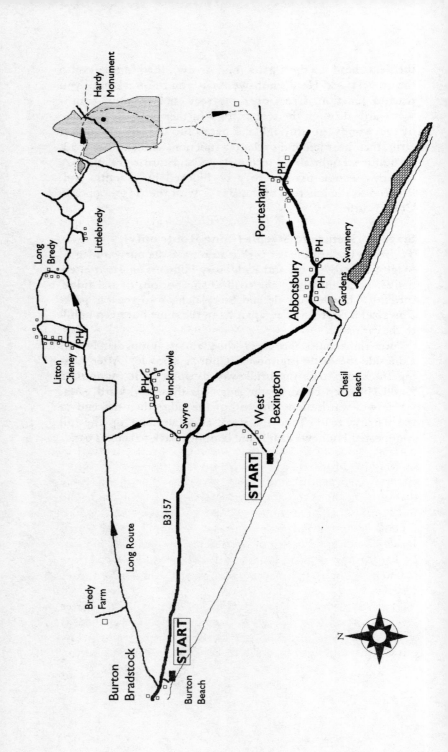

RIDE 14

HARDY'S MONUMENT

Short Route: 16 miles, 2½ hours
Long Route: 23 miles, 3½ hours

Route Description

This ride is based around the Dorset hills above Chesil Beach, just to the north of Weymouth. The route is over open downs and there are some superb views of the coastline from the hills.

Hardy's Monument is one of the aims for this ride and it is worth the uphill to the monument for the views to Portland. It is actually a memorial not to Thomas Hardy, as one might expect, but to Admiral Hardy, of Trafalgar fame. The village of Abbotsbury is good for sightseeing. Not only is it picturesque, it also has the Swannery and Sub-Tropical Gardens. There is a slight detour to the scenic village of Littlebredy, to view the source of the river Bride. Burton Beach, at the start of the long route, is probably the best beach in the area. Owned by the National Trust, it has clean coarse sand, and is suitable for swimming.

Bridleways in this area tend to be unmarked and overgrown, making them difficult to use in the ride. This has resulted in quite a high proportion of this ride on road, although the quiet country lanes used on the routes provide good cycling. Note that once off the beaten track they are not well signposted. The tracks around Hardy's monument are well defined and there is a good descent from the monument. The track along Chesil Beach allows good views of this interesting coastline, but can be hard going if there is a westerly headwind. The ride encounters two steep uphill sections, at West Bexington and from Littlebredy.

There are plenty of places to eat in Abbotsbury. The Ilchester Arms and the Swan Inn both serve good food, and there is also a Tea Rooms in the village. There are further pubs at Litton Cheney and Portesham. Both West Bexington and Burton

67

beaches have cafes which serve tea and snacks.

In order to make Hardy's Monument a common objective to both routes, I have varied the start points to achieve suitable distances.

Start Short Route (OS Landranger Sheet 194. Grid reference 532864)

The start point for this route is the beach car park at West Bexington. From Bridport take the B3157 towards Weymouth. About 5 miles from Bridport, at Swyre, is a turn to your right (signposted West Bexington). Take this turn and proceed downhill to the beach, where the car park is ahead of you. Note that since it is necessary to cycle back up the hill you have just driven down, you may wish to drop some people and gear off at Swyre and appoint one of the more fit members of the party to cycle back up the hill!

Start Long Route (OS Landranger Sheet 194. Grid reference 492887)

The start point for this route is the beach car park at Burton Bradstock. From Bridport take the B3157 towards Weymouth, and after about 2 miles you will reach Burton Bradstock. At the far end of the village, turn right to Burton Beach (black National Trust signpost , To Burton Beach). The car park is to your left at the beach, and will cost you around £1.00.

Stage 1 To Litton Cheney

The first part of the ride is to cycle via the Bride valley to Litton Cheney. Since there are two different starting points, the directions for this are given in the following sections:

Short Route

From the car park cycle back up the hill through West Bexington. The first part of the hill is steep, but after the road bears left, the incline is easier. When you reach the B3157 at Swyre, turn left then almost immediately right (signposted Puncknowle). Continue on this road for ½ mile and just after the road bends sharp right before entering Puncknowle, turn left down a hill. At the junction at the bottom of the hill, turn right and cycle to the White Horse pub on the outskirts of Litton Cheney.

Long Route
From the car park cycle back to Burton Bradstock. When you reach the B3157 again, turn left then almost immediately right (signposted Litton Cheney). Continue on this road for about 4 miles, following the river, until you reach the White Horse pub on the outskirts of Litton Cheney.

Stage 2   Hardy's Monument
At Litton Cheney, turn right on the narrow metalled road immediately before the pub and proceed along the road for about a mile. Just after the road bends left into Long Bredy, turn right to Littlebredy. Cycle along the foot of a ridge through park-like surroundings above the river until you reach the outskirts of Littlebredy. Turn right for a short excursion down to the village centre.

Return to the road, and proceed out of the village. After a short distance, take the right fork which will lead you up a steep hill ½ mile further on . At the junction at the top of the hill, turn right. A short distance on, where the verge on your left opens out, turn left down a path. This bridleway follows round the edge of a field to a road. Cross the road to a better defined track opposite that leads into the woods. Keep heading westwards through the woods until you emerge onto a road. Hardy's Monument is a few hundred yards uphill to your right, and it is worth the effort to visit the monument for the views.

Stage 3   Portesham and Abbotsbury
From Hardy's Monument, return to where you came out of the wood onto the road, and cross to a gravel track opposite. Take the right hand fork and follow the edge of the wood around the hill, below the monument. You will reach an open grassy area in a dip, from which a number of tracks radiate (all signposted Bridleway). Bear left down to the gate by the stone wall. Go through the gate and proceed uphill along by the wall. Near the top of the hill, take the left fork and pass by a farm, then bear right and descend to the road. At the road, turn right and

cycle to the T Junction. Turn left and descend to the B3157 at Portesham.

Turn right and cycle down the B3157 towards Abbotsbury. At the end of Portesham village is a gravel driveway to your right, down which a bridleway leads (unsignposted). Turn right here towards some houses and go to the end of the track. The bridleway continues along the path of the old railway that lies ahead. Follow the railway line through some gates until it emerges onto the B3157. Turn right and cycle into Abbotsbury.

Stage 4   Return from Abbotsbury

Follow the B3157 through Abbotsbury towards Bridport, and where the road bends right up a hill go straight on down a minor road (signposted Tropical Gardens). Follow this road down to the beach, where it turns right and deteriorates into a track. Cycle for 2 miles parallel to the sea, on the gravel track behind the beach. You will then reach the car park at West Bexington.

Long Route

At the car park, turn right and cycle up the hill through West Bexington. The first part of the hill is steep, but after the road bears left, the incline is easier. When you reach the B3157 at Swyre, turn left then almost immediately right (signposted Puncknowle). Continue on this road for ½ mile and just after the road bends sharp right before entering Puncknowle, turn left down a hill. At the junction at the bottom of the hill, turn left and cycle back to the outskirts of Burton Bradstock. At the T junction, turn left then almost immediately right, back to the car park at Burton Beach.

RIDE 15

CERNE ABBAS

Long Route: 18 miles, 3½ hours

Route Description

This is a ride for the more energetic cyclist, providing some excellent views over open hills in a popular walking area around Cerne Abbas. For sightseeing, there is the attraction of the Cerne Abbas Giant, carved in the chalk hillside to the north of the village.

This is not a ride for the faint-hearted! There are some extremely steep hills on the route and which ever way you cycle you will encounter 5 steep uphills. The direction I have chosen for this ride is to cycle/walk up the shortest, steepest uphills and descend on the longer downhills. Most of the ride is off-road, but the bridleways in this area are poorly marked and route finding can be difficult. Since this is a ride for the off-road enthusiast I have used some less well defined bridleway sections. You will also encounter a number of gates (of varying degrees of difficulty) on this ride.

There are two good pubs on the route. The Brace of Pheasants at Plush serves good but expensive food, while the Gaggle of Geese at Buckland Newton provides a good range of meals and snacks at reasonable prices. There also are plenty of places to eat in Cerne Abbas though the village can become busy with tourist traffic in summer.

Start   (OS Landranger Sheet 194. Grid reference 636039)

From Dorchester take the A352 towards Sherborne. Continue past Cerne Abbas and after a further 2½ miles take a left turn (signposted Evershot). Proceed uphill and along the top you will find the car park on your right (signposted Batcombe Picnic Area).

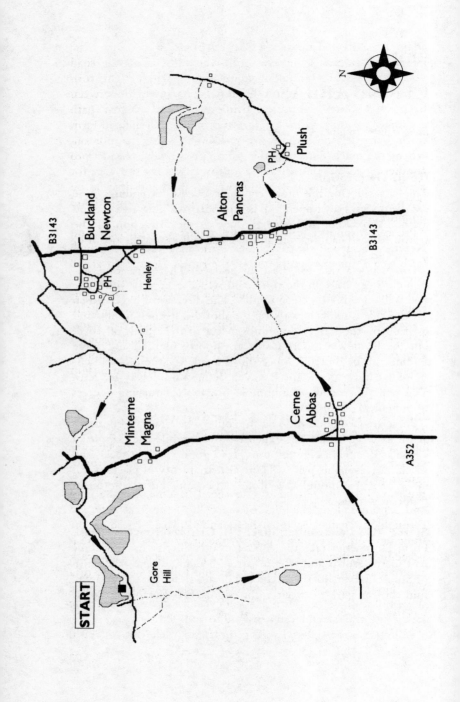

Stage 1   Alton Pancras via Cerne Abbas.

From the car park, continue south-westwards along the road you have just driven along until you reach a right turn (signposted The Friary). Turn left down a narrow path between hedges, opposite (signposted Bridleway). This narrow path continues for only ½ mile before meeting a well defined farm track. Turn left onto the farm track and another ½ mile on, where the track bends to the right, go straight ahead onto another track. Continue heading southwards along the ridge for about 2 miles until you meet a road. Turn left and descend on the road to the A352 at Cerne Abbas. Cross the main road and go into the village centre opposite.

Proceed through Cerne Abbas following signs for Buckland Newton. You will shortly come to the first steep hill, which leads to a T junction at the top of the ridge. Go straight ahead over the T junction to a grass path in the field opposite (unsignposted). Pass through the field, through a gate, then continue along the edge of another field until you reach a barn. Take the right fork and proceed downhill along a farm track. Where the track bends sharp right go straight ahead through a gate to a narrow path. Descend with the path to some houses and go through the gate to the B3143 ahead of you. Turn right along the B3143 into Alton Pancras.

Stage 2   Alton Pancras to Buckland Newton

Opposite the entrance to the church, turn left through a gate onto a track in a grass field. Here the path of the bridleway is well defined and runs up the hill ahead of you. Proceed uphill, ignoring the right fork, until you reach an open grassy area at the top. Take the left-hand gate ahead of you into the field and continue along the edge of the field to the next gate. Go through this gate into open heathland. Proceed ahead in the direction you were travelling, over the brow of the hill (there is no defined path here), until you meet a perpendicular grass track running along the ridge. Turn right and follow the ridge to a gate. Go through the gate to a more-defined track and continue downhill to the road. Turn left and cycle into Plush, where the Brace of Pheasants pub can be found to your left.

Follow the road round to the right and cycle out of Plush.

Just over a mile further along this road you will come to Folly Farmhouse. Turn left (signposted Bridleway to Alton Pancras) and proceed uphill on the track. Towards the top of the hill, the track ends in a grassy field. Continue ahead to the wood where you will meet a gate. Go through the gate into the wood and bear right onto a track. The track emerges from the wood (through another gate) to a grassy area. There is a faintly discernable path across the field which you should follow: it bears left and runs westwards alongside the wooded area to a gate in the top left corner. Pass through the gate onto a track and descend to the B3143.

Turn right and cycle up the road for about a mile. Take a left turn (signposted Henley) and continue on this road to the T junction in Buckland Newton. Turn left, and to your left is the Gaggle of Geese pub.

Stage 3   Return from Buckland Newton

Continue a few hundred yards down the road passed the pub and take the next road to your left (unsignposted apart from no through road sign). Keep straight on until you reach Knap Farm. Go through the farm entrance (there may be information posted on the bridleway) and turn right along a narrow path (signposted Bridleway to Matis Hill). This path may be overgrown and muddy for a short distance, but it soon opens into a track as it ascends the steep hill. Continue on the track until it meets the road at a layby. Turn right and cycle along the road. Where the road starts to go down a hill, turn sharp left down a track (unsignposted except for Unsuitable for Motor Vehicles sign), and follow this track for 1½ miles until it reaches the A352. Turn left along the main road then take a right turn (signposted Evershot) along the road you drove up to the car park on. Continue uphill, then along the ridge until you return to the car park.

IBBERTON DOWN AND THE RIVER STOUR

Long Route: 16 – 18 miles, 3 hours

Route Description

This ride follows an almost totally off-road route to the west of Blandford Forum, descending from Ibberton Down to the river Stour. Although the bridleways used are of a good standard, this is one of the more rugged routes.

The ride provides a wealth of sights for those interested interested in history and archaeology. There is the Roman hill fort at Hod Hill, an Iron Age hill fort at Hambledon Hill, and an ancient settlement at Ringmoor administered by the National Trust. There are fine views from the Roman hill fort at Hod Hill, and it is worth a detour up to view the monument, which is remarkably well preserved. If you do go into the monument, please leave your bike locked to the entrance gate; mountain bikers have been receiving bad publicity for damage caused to some areas, so cycling around this ancient site will not be appreciated.

There are 2 good off-road sections over Ibberton Down, but probably the best section is the superb bridleway right beside the river Stour. The route is not generally muddy, apart from the section by the river. There is one steep uphill section from Okeford Fitzpaine, but it is not that long, flattening out in the middle. Shillingstone is an unattractive sprawl along the A357 busy with lorries from the nearby chalk quarry, and is best avoided. Because of this I have used a disused railway track, popular with local walkers, to provide a detour.

The White Horse pub at Stourpaine serves food, and there are plenty of possible picnic stops along by the river Stour. The Saxon Inn at Child Okeford, a typical village pub noted for both its' food and ambiance, is a short distance off the route.

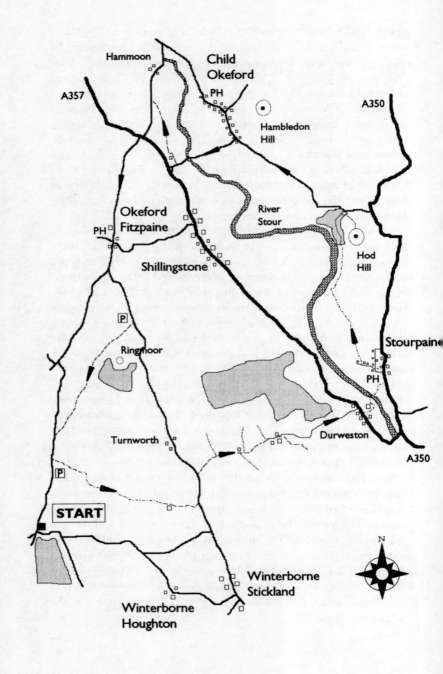

Start   (OS Landranger Sheet 194. Grid reference 786062)

From Blandford Forum, take the A354 towards Dorchester. At Winterborne Whitechurch, take a right turn (signposted Winterborne Stickland). At Winterborne Stickland take the second left turn (signposted Winterborne Houghton) and continue into the village of Winterborne Houghton. Bear right with the road (ahead is no through road), and drive uphill to a junction with a more major road. Turn left and drive to the top of the hill, where you will come to a crossroads. Turn sharp right and the car park area is on your right.

Note that you can also park further along the ridge at Ibberton Hill Picnic Site, thereby shortening the ride by almost 2 miles. However, the terrain at this site is uneven.

Stage 1   Across Ibberton Down to Stourpaine

From the car park, cycle north–eastwards on the road along the ridge until you reach Ibberton Hill Picnic Site to your right. Halfway along the site is a gravel track (signposted Bridleway, from the road). Turn right down this track and continue until you come to a gate. Go through the gate into the field and turn right. Follow the dark blue arrows around the edge of the field until you reach a farm track. Proceed downhill on this track until you come to a road.

Turn left and cycle a short distance along the road until you see a track on your right (signposted Bridleway to Durweston). Turn right and go uphill on this track, ignoring any turnings. After just over a mile you will reach a group of houses. Take the narrow metalled road that lies ahead to your left and cycle downhill to the A357 at Durweston.

Turn right along the main road and after a few hundred yards turn left down a road (marked Private Road). Though there is no evidence of the right of way from the main road, a bridleway runs down this driveway, as you will discover at the end. Where the driveway ends at the river, turn left behind a building to a narrow metal gate. Go through the gate and bear right towards the river. Cross the river via a green metal bridge, pass under the railway bridge and follow the bridleway uphill to the A350 at Stourpaine. Turn left along the main road until you come to the White Horse pub.

Stage 2   Along the River Stour

Take a left turn immediately after the White Horse pub into Stourpaine (named South Holme). At the crossroads go ahead (named Havelins) and a little further on turn right towards Hod Hill (signposted Bridleway to Hanford). Proceed up a slight incline beneath the hill fort until you enter a wooded area by the river. This is an excellent area for a picnic, but as you would expect beside a river, it can be muddy. Follow alongside the river, then bear right with the path to a road. To you right is a bridleway ascending to the hill fort on Hod Hill. Turn left and cycle along the road for 2 miles to Child Okeford.

At Child Okeford, turn left (signposted Shillingstone). (For the Saxon Inn, continue ahead downhill through Child Okeford and the pub is at the end of the village, tucked away on your right). Cross the river Stour and shortly after turn right (signposted Bridleway to Hammoon) along a narrow road to a farm. Pass the farm shop (which sells ice cream!) then turn left immediately behind a barn to join up with the disused railway track. Cycle along the railway track for a mile until you reach a road, then turn left and return to the A357.

Stage 3   Return over Ibberton Down

At the crossroads with the A357, take the road ahead (signposted Okeford Fitzpaine) and proceed straight on through the village of Okeford Fitzpaine. About ½ mile after the centre of Okeford Fitzpaine, turn left (signposted Turnworth). You now have to ascend the steep hill ahead, although the road does level off halfway up before becoming steep again just before the summit. At the top of the hill is Okeford Hill car park (signposted Picnic Area), at the end of which is a track crossing (unsignposted). Turn right up the track and proceed up the incline to the top of the hill. Ringmoor settlement is to your left as you ascend. Follow the track downhill to the road, turn left and cycle on the road along the ridge until you come back to where you parked the car.

RIDE 17

BADBURY RINGS

Short Route: 16 miles, 2½ hours
Long Route: 22 miles, 3½ hours

Route Description

This ride starts at the ancient hill fort of Badbury Rings, passes through the surrounding countryside, returning along by the river Stour. Badbury Rings is an iron age hill fort consisting of three sections of ramparts (hence the term "rings") on a small hill above the river Stour. It is worth a walk up to the fort for an inspection of these impressive earthworks. The long route does a complete circumnavigation of the Rings.

The cycling is through fairly flat terrain. There is only one hill on the route, downhill to the river Tarrant, but this does mean that the bridleway section from Manswood is up an incline for just over a mile. There are three good bridleway sections on this ride. The surfaces are good and since there are no muddy sections, the route can be cycled in quite wet weather. In two places the bridleways become quite narrow for short sections, but since they are regularly used this should not cause a problem.

There is one pub on the route, The Lovers Knot at Tarrant Keyneston which serves food.

Start   (OS Landranger Sheet 195. Grid reference 962032)

From Blandford Forum, take the B3082 towards Wimborne Minster. On your left, about 5 miles from Blandford, is the entrance to Badbury Rings (historical signpost). Go up the track to the National Trust car park just below the Rings.

Stage 1   Out from the Rings

Take the track from the lower corner of the car park, in a north-easterly direction past the Rings. Cycle alongside the fence and uphill into a wood. Where a track intersects, proceed across to the least-defined track, offset slightly to your left. Continue on this track until it emerges from the wood, then turn left down a

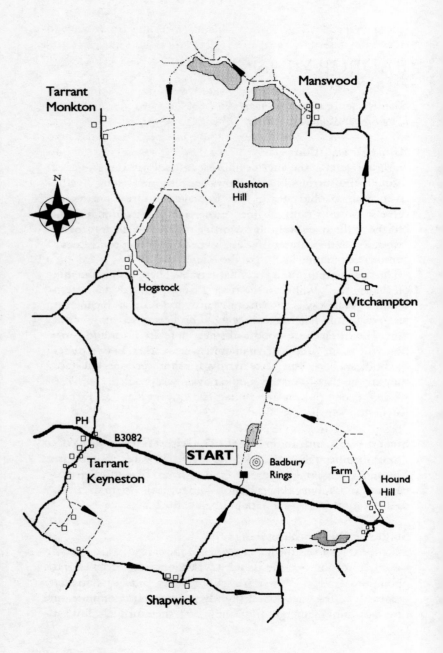

more defined track. Go downhill and where this track bends to the right, take the grassy track that lies ahead. This becomes quite narrow for a short distance then opens out again before reaching the road.

At the road go straight ahead and cycle for about a mile until you reach a crossroads. Take the road ahead (signposted Moor Crichel) and continue along this road, ignoring any right turns to Witchampton. At a sharp right hand bend, take the road ahead of you (signposted Manswood). At the next junction turn right down to Manswood, and at the bottom of the hill turn left down a track (signposted Bridleway to Turners Vine).

Follow the track to the right and pass through some gates. Cycle for about a mile until you reach the intersection of 4 tracks. Take the right fork ahead of you and cycle in a north-westerly direction up a hill. The track does a left wheel round a wood, and you should keep bearing left until you are along a ridge overlooking Tarrant Monkton. Carry on along the ridge until you reach a grassy opening.

Go through the gate in the left hand corner and proceed along a grassy track. The surface can be quite lumpy, but it is only for a short distance. At the edge of the wood you will meet another track. Bear right at this intersection, then bear left at the next intersection, keeping along the edge of the wood. Continue onto a metalled surface past some houses until you meet a road.

Stage 2   The two rivers

At the junction turn right, back on yourself. Cycle to the top of the hill, then downhill and over the river Tarrant. Continue along the road keeping the river to your left until you meet the B3082 at Tarrant Keyneston. To your right is The Lovers Knot pub.

Cross the B3082 to the road opposite and cycle through the village. At the end of the village you will find yourself alongside the river. On your left is a small bridge with a path crossing the river (signposted Bridleway to Tarrant Crawford). Take the bridleway across the river. This is quite narrow but it soon meets up with a more defined track, where you should turn left and cycle up the hill. Bear right with the track and descend to the road, where you turn left. After a mile you will reach Shapwick, with the river Stour to your right. Go through the village until you come to a junction by the war memorial and church.

Stage 3   Return to Badbury

Depending on your choice of routes, there are two ways to return to Badbury Rings.

Short Route

At the junction turn left and cycle up to the B3082. Opposite you is the entrance to the car park at Badbury Rings.

Long Route

At the junction continue straight on. After 1½ miles you will come to a T junction. To your right is the river Stour, and it is worth a detour down to the river for the views. Turn left and cycle uphill until you come to a left turn (signposted Shapwick). Take the bridleway to your right, opposite, (signposted Bridleway). Continue along the bridleway, bearing right around a wood, until you meet a road. Turn left at the road and proceed to the B3082. Cross to the road opposite (signposted Hound Hill). After a mile the road becomes a track, and at the next junction of tracks, continue straight across. To your left are views of Badbury Rings. A mile further on the track bears sharp left. You may recognise that this is the track you cycled out on. Proceed uphill and turn right through the wood to arrive back at the car park.

PENTRIDGE HILL

Long Route (1): 18 miles, 3½ hours
Long Route (2): 22 miles, 4 hours

Route Description

This is a challenging route around downland to the west of
Salisbury, comprising of two loops to the north and south of
Cranborne. There are a number of archaelogical sites on the
ride, including cycling along the line of Bokerley Ditch (con-
structed in the late Roman period to protect against invaders)
and along the route of the old Roman road of Ackling Dyke.

There is an excellent ride along the ridge of Pentridge Hill,
with fine views over the surrounding countryside, and also
good descents from Blagdon Hill and from Hartley Down. The
tracks are mainly rough and grassy, making it hard cycling. On
the north loop, route-finding across Pentridge Hill is difficult,
but the south loop is easier. The route has been arranged to get
the best gradients, and to make route finding easiest. There is
only one uphill of note, the climb to Pentridge Hill from
Cranborne. Considering the height gained the rise is surprisingly gentle, but the rough grassy track makes it hard going.

The Drovers Inn at Gussage All Saints is a good village pub
which serves bar food. There is a general stores in Cranborne
together with 2 further pubs.

Start   (OS Landranger Sheets 184, 195. Grid ref 025154)

From Salisbury take the A354 towards Blandford Forum.
About 12 miles from Salisbury, at a roundabout where the
B3081 intersects, turn left onto the B3081 (signposted Wimborne Minster). On either side of the road you will see that the
wide verges have been used for informal car parking (in summer
this is a popular picnic area). Drive along the road for about 1
mile, then choose a suitable parking point nearest possible to
Cranborne. The best parking is by a wooded area on your right.
If you park on the verge, be careful of the raised edges, using

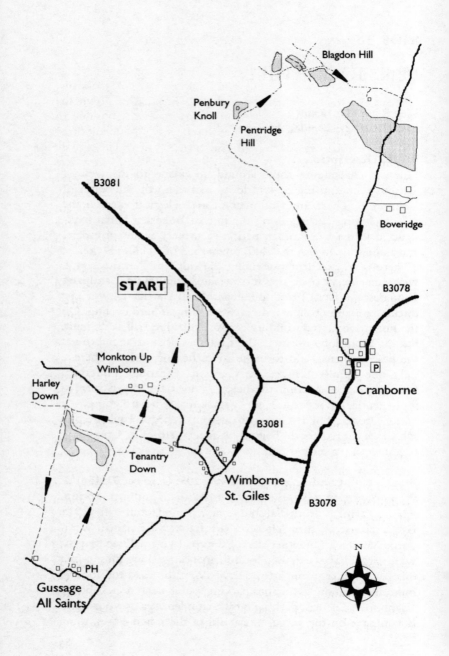

one of the narrow "entrances" to get on to them.

Stage 1   To Pentridge Hill

Cycle south-eastwards along the B3081 towards Cranborne.
Where the road bends sharply to your right, turn down the
minor road to your left (signposted Cranborne). Continue to
the crossroads then turn left on the B3078 into Cranborne.
Where the road bends sharp right, turn left into The Square
(signposted Boveridge) and take the road ahead of you that
bears right. After ½ mile take a narrow road that forks to your
left (signposted Bridleway to Pentridge). At the end of this road,
pass through a gate onto a grassy track. This track leads up to
the top of Pentridge Hill 2½ miles away. As you approach the
top of the ridge, the climb steepens and the track appears to end
in a grassy area between fences.

Bear to your right and go through the narrow gate situated
between hedges. On the other side of the gate you will find
yourself in a grass field with only a faintly discernable path.
Head north-eastwards towards the clump of trees (Penbury
Knoll), following the right hand fence along the top of the
ridge. From here there are fine views across Cranborne Chase.
On reaching Penbury Knoll, go through the gate into the
wooded area. The blue arrow on the gate reassures you that you
are on a marked track! The outline of this hill fort is now barely
visible, and the track through it is rutted and can be muddy.

Emerge from the wood onto open grass again. Head north-
eastwards along the ridge for a distance of ½ mile, which now
gives views to your right over Cranborne. At this stage you
need to be diligent to avoid getting lost. The course of the bridleway follows the contour of the summit round to your left, but
is difficult to see. Rather misleading is the clump of trees ahead
of you with a gate in the fence. Ignore this gate and turn to
your left, heading due north downhill parallel to the fence. Aim
towards the wooded area situated half-way down the hill, and
as you approach this wood you will notice a narrow gate on
your right which gives access to a path between hedgerows. Go
through this gate onto a well-worn narrow path. This is popular
with walkers, so be vigilant. The path leads eastwards into a
wooded area, then through a gate onto a well defined track.

Turn right onto the track then take the next track on your left and go out of the woods. From here you will see the line of Bokerley Ditch over Martin Down, to your left. Cross over the ditch and turn right onto the grassy path to the summit of Blagdon Hill. At the top of the hill, follow the line of the track ahead over the ditch, then bear right and follow the narrow path downhill through bushes. This is a good downhill section, but be aware that the mud surface can be slippy. Fortunately, this route is not so popular with walkers, so you should have it to yourself. Pass through a gate into a small enclosure, then through another gate to your left.

Here the path runs out and you are left in a grass field. The bridleway follows a line to the right of the trees on the brow, parallel with the right hand fence, down to a gate. Go through the gate onto a farm track and turn left. Cycle along the farm track to a junction with a minor metalled road. Turn right along the road and cycle back to Cranborne. This quiet country lane makes a pleasing contrast with the rough terrain of the last few miles.

Stage 2 Tenantry and Harley Downs
From Cranborne square turn right onto the B3078 (signposted Wimborne). Cycle out of Cranborne for 1 mile before taking a right turn onto the B3081 (signposted Shaftesbury). Just under a mile further on, take a turn down a more minor road to your left (signposted Wimborne St Giles). Continue into Wimborne St Giles, over the bridge then take an almost immediate right turn (signposted Monkton Up Wimborne). Just under a mile from the turn, where the road bends sharp right by a white house, take the concrete road ahead that leads into a farm (unsignposted). This bridleway becomes a loose gravel track after the farm as it ascends to Tenantry Down.

At the top of the down you are confronted with a staggered crossroads of tracks (signposted with blue arrows).

Long Route (1)
Follow the main track right then keep straight ahead (blue arrow) onto a grassy track. This route now continues from Stage 3.

Long Route (2)

Follow the main track right then left to continue north-westwards up to Harley Down. The loose gravel gives way to a firmer surface, easing the ascent. Towards the top of Harley Down, you enter a wooded area. Ignore the first bridleway to your left (blue arrow) and continue a further 100 yards until you emerge from the woods at the top of the down. From here there are good views back across to Pentridge Hill. Turn left onto the grassy track before the gravestone of John Ironmonger. The route now follows the course of the Roman road Ackling Dyke downhill for 2 miles to a metalled road. After a slight initial climb, this becomes a fast descent but beware of the single bar gate strategically placed at head height 100 yards before the road!

At the road, turn left and cycle into Gussage All Saints. Bear left with the road over the stream and where the road bears right continue straight ahead up a no through road by the War Memorial. (The Drovers Inn is ½ mile further into the village).

At the end of the no through road, go round a white single bar gate onto a gravel track. Follow this track for a mile, then bear right up a steeper incline. At the top bear left and continue back to the staggered crossroads at Tenantry Down. Go onto the main track, but this time keep straight ahead (blue arrow) onto a grassy track.

Stage 3   Return from Tenantry Down

Descend on the grassy track to a road. Turn right onto the road then 200 yards on take a bridleway to your left (blue arrow). The grassy track goes uphill, levelling off with some good sweeping bends, before entering woodland. You will emerge from the woods past a white single bar gate onto the B3081. Turn left to where you parked the car.

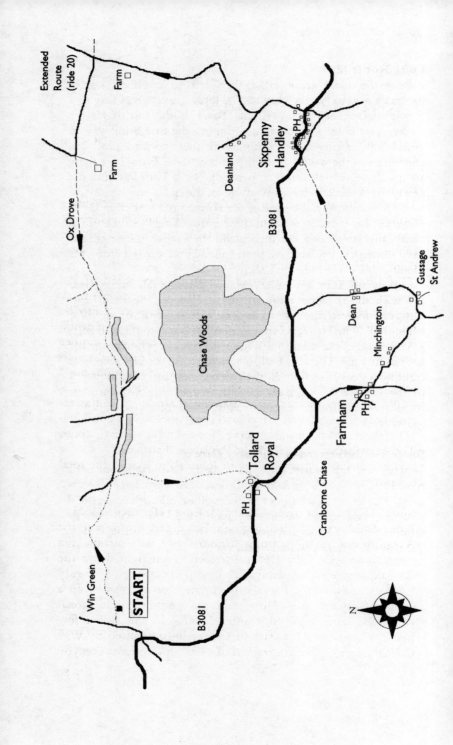

RIDE 19

CRANBORNE CHASE

Long Route: 18 miles, 3 hours
Extended Route: 36 miles, 6 hours

Route Description

This ride follows a route through Cranborne Chase and along a chalk ridge, between Salisbury and Blandford Forum. There are good views from the uplands at Win Green (it is alleged that one can see to the Isle of Wight on a clear day) and the ride passes through the well kept parkland of the Chase.

The bridleways over the chalk hills are of good standard, the descent to Tollard Royal being excellent. The grassy track of the Ox Drove provides good cycling, however it can be muddy in places, depending on recent weather. There is a gentle country lane section through Cranborne Chase, and another bridleway section to Sixpenny Handley that passes through farmland. There is one uphill section of 1 mile duration, but I have chosen the least steep return to the ridge.

Unfortunately the village of Sixpenny Handley is not as attractive as it's name suggests. However it does have a good pub (The Roebuck Inn) which serves food, and a general stores. There are further pubs at Tollard Royal and Farnham.

This ride can be combined with Ride 20 to extend the total distance up to 36 miles.

Start (OS Landranger Sheet 184. Grid reference 924205)

From Salisbury, proceed towards Blandford Forum on the A354. About 12 miles from Salisbury you will encounter a roundabout where the B3081 intersects. Turn right down the B3081 (signposted Sixpenny Handley). Pass through Sixpenny Handley and Tollard Royal and continue on the B3081 up a steep hill to Charlton Down. At the summit is a diagonal crossroads. Turn right (signposted Donheads) and after a few hundred yards there is a track to your right (signposted By Way to Win Green). Take this track, and a few hundred yards on you will come to a National Trust car park.

Stage 1   Descent to Tollard Royal

From the car park take the track alongside the National Trust sign in a north-easterly direction. Cycle over the summit past the trig point, then downhill onto a chalk track. Continue on this track until you come to a junction alongside a metalled road. Take the right fork (signposted "By Way to Tollard Royal"). Bear right with the track and descend for 2 miles to Tollard Royal. At the B3081, turn left towards Sixpenny Handley.

Stage 2   On to Sixpenny Handley

About 1 mile from Tollard Royal, where the B3081 bends to the left, take a right turn (signposted Farnham). At the outskirts of Farnham, continue straight on ignoring a turn to your right (signposted Farnham). Take the next turn to your left, a short distance along by a farm (unsignposted). Continue to a T junction, then turn left to Gussage St Andrew and proceed to Dean. Note that not all of these places are signposted, but by continually taking a left turn around the loop, you should not find this a problem (if you meet the A354 you have not taken enough left turns!).

At Dean (a mile from the left turn that led you to Gussage St Andrew) take a track to your right (signposted Bridleway, with light blue marker). Continue on this track to the outskirts of Sixpenny Handley. At the junction with the road, take the B3081 ahead of you into the village. The Roebuck Inn is halfway through the village, on your left.

Stage 3   Return via the Ox Drove

At the end of Sixpenny Handley, turn left (signposted Deanland). After ½ mile take the right fork and continue uphill (the left fork is a no through road to Deanland). At the top of the hill you will come to a junction, with a road to your left and the Ox Drove to your right. (**Extended Route:** continue downhill on the road through Bowerchalke to Broad Chalke. This will meet up with Ride 20 (at Stage 2). Ride 20 extended route will give you directions back to Win Green.)

Take the road on your left, which forms part of the Ox Drove at this stage, and cycle along the ridge. Continue for about a mile until you come to a point where the road bears sharp right, and to your left is West Chase Farm. Proceed straight across onto the track ahead of you (signposted By Way to Ox Drove). After 2½ miles the track meets up with a metalled road again. Continue ahead on the road, along the ridge. Just before the road starts downhill, you will come alongside the track you took to Tollard Royal. Follow the track westwards back to the car park (signposted By Way to Win Green).

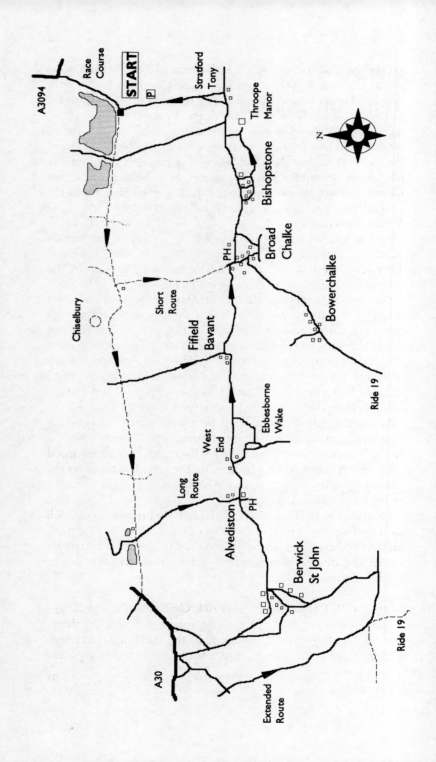

RIDE 20

THE EBBLE VALLEY

Short Route (1): 12 miles, 2 hours
Short Route (2): 16 miles, 2½ hours
Long Route: 21 miles, 3½ hours
Extended Route: 36 miles, 6 hours

Route Description

This ride follows an off-road route along a ridge to the west of Salisbury, returning via the quiet road in the valley below. There are excellent views of the surrounding hills from the ridge, and the ride passes through the picturesque Ebble Valley.

There are regular opportunities for leaving the track along the ridge to transfer to the valley road, thereby allowing you to chose a suitable distance. The start of the ride can be wet as it passes through woodland, though this dries out after 6 miles even in the worst conditions. The valley road is designated as a Wiltshire Cycle Way and passes through a number of small villages. Since the ridge is rather exposed, I would not recommend cycling this route if there is a strong westerly wind.

Along the Ebble Valley are plenty of small villages for sightseeing, with pubs for refreshment. The Queens Head at Broad Chalke is a well-furnished village pub that serves good food, and is common to all routes on the ride. For those on the long route The Crown Inn at Alvediston is a good pub that serves food, earlier in the ride.

This ride can be combined with Ride 19 to provide a good full days cycling over a total distance of 36 miles. Note that the track on the southern ridge of the valley (the Ox Drove) is extremely rutted and muddy at the eastern end, so it is advisable not to detour to this.

Start   (OS Landranger Sheet 184. Grid reference 093286)

From Salisbury centre, take the ring road and follow the directions for A36 towards Warminster. At the traffic lights between Quidhampton and Wilton, turn left on the A3094 (signposted

Race Course). Where the A3094 bends sharply left, take the road straight ahead (signposted Race Course). Continue uphill past the Race Course, until the road bends left. On your right at the bend is the start of the ride. There are a few places to park at the start point (entrance to Hare Warren Wood), or if these are taken, there is a layby a few hundred yards further down the road, past the bend.

Stage 1   Along the ridge

From the start point cycle along the track on the edge of the wood in a westerly direction. Since this section is a BOAT, open to all traffic, you may have to give way for vehicles to pass. The surface is semi-metalled and can be quite harsh and wet, but this does mean it has the benefit of not being too rutted. After just under a mile of cycling, you will meet a crossroads with a metalled road. Carry straight on across the road into another wooded area, where the surface becomes more like a track.

You should continue heading westwards along the track, ignoring turns to your left or right until you decide to descend to the valley. Be aware that the track along the ridge does not always appear as the major one.

Short Route (1)

After about 5 miles from the start point, the track joins a bridleway coming from the right, with a gravel surface. This then turns left, becoming a bridleway leading down to Broad Chalke. Follow the directions later in the ride from Broad Chalke (Stage 2).

Short Route (2)

Continue westwards to the top of the down, where there are earthworks (Chiselbury and the Regimental carvings). About 7 miles from the start point, you will meet a crossroads with metalled road. Turn left onto the road and descend to Fifield Bavant. At the T junction, turn left onto the valley road and cycle to Broad Chalke. Follow the directions later in the ride from Broad Chalke (Stage 2).

Long Route

Continue westwards along the ridge, past Chiselbury fort and across the road that descends to Fifield Bavant. From here on the surface becomes progressively drier, turning into a gravel and chalk track. About 10 miles from the start point you will come to another crossroads with a metalled road, by a white building on the edge of a wood. Leave the track by turning left and descend on the road to Alvediston. Ahead of you at the T junction in Alvediston is the Crown Inn.

At Alvediston, turn left along the valley road towards Salisbury and after about a mile bear left at West End. (The right turn leads into Ebbesborne Wake, then back to the valley road). Two miles further on from West End, bear left then right at Fifield Bavant to stay on the valley road. After cycling for another 1½ miles you will reach Broad Chalke. Follow the directions later in the ride from Broad Chalke (Stage 2).

Extended Route

Continue westwards along the ridge, past Chiselbury fort and across the road that descends to Fifield Bavant, until you reach the road to Alvediston. Carry on across the road into the wood ahead. After about 2 miles the track descends through a steep cutting to the A30. Be careful of the loose and slippery chalk surface on this descent. At the A30, turn left and take the second turn to your left, (signposted Berwick St John). Take an immediate right, then a left at the next crossroads and up a hill, on narrow metalled roads. This will meet up with Ride 19 at the "By Way to Tollard Royal" signpost. Ride 19 extended route will give you directions back to the valley road at Broad Chalke (see page 90).

Stage 2   Return from Broad Chalke

On entering Broad Chalke, The Queens Head is to your left, opposite the river. Proceed eastwards from Broad Chalke along the road on the north bank of the River Ebble until Bishopstone. Take the third right turn in Bishopstone, then turn next left over the river and cycle along the south bank. This is a pleasant narrow lane that follows along the course of the river.

At the road junction by Throope Manor, turn left across the river back to the valley road, and turn right. On entering Stratford Tony, turn left, then left at the next junction, and cycle uphill back to the car.